THE VEGAN DIVAS
COOKBOOK

THE VEGAN DIVAS
COOKBOOK

Delicious Desserts, Plates, and Treats
from the Famed New York City Bakery

FERNANDA CAPOBIANCO

HARPER WAVE

HarperCollins books may be purchased for educational, business, or sales promotional use. For information, please e-mail the Special Markets Department at SPsales@harpercollins.com.

FIRST EDITION

Designed by Leah Carlson-Stanisic

Photographs by Rogério Voltan

Library of Congress Cataloging-in-Publication Data has been applied for.

ISBN: 978-0-06-224483-3

13 14 15 16 17   ov/QGT   10 9 8 7 6 5 4 3 2 1

DEDICATION

I dedicate this book to my mom and best friend, SUELY CAPOBIANCO, and to my brother, MARCUS CAPOBIANCO—my greatest role models in life, who supported me when I moved to New York in 2009 and started this exciting journey. Also, to MARCUS CAPOBIANCO, my dad, who had a fun life and who made me realize that our health is the biggest treasure we have.

CONTENTS

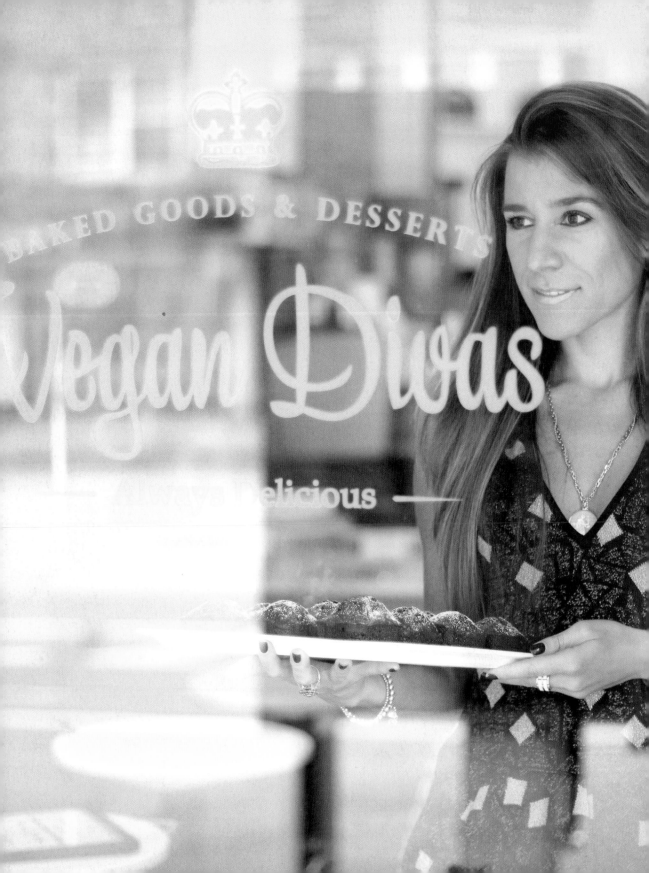

INTRODUCTION

HOW I BECAME A VEGAN DIVA

BORN AND RAISED IN BRAZIL, A COUNTRY KNOWN FOR CATTLE RANCHING AND WHERE BEEF IS USED IN MANY POPULAR DISHES, I AM AN UNLIKELY VEGAN. FROM THE TIME I WAS A CHILD, I REJECTED MEAT—I HATED ITS TASTE AND TEXTURE AND REFUSED TO EAT IT EVEN WHEN, EVERY SUNDAY, MY WHOLE FAMILY HEADED OFF TO THE LOCAL *CHURRASCARIA* FOR A CARNIVORE'S FEAST. THANKFULLY, MY PARENTS NEVER FORCED ME TO EAT MEAT, BUT THEY DID TAKE ME TO SEE A NUTRITIONIST TO HELP ME REPLACE THE PROTEIN I WASN'T GETTING IN MY DIET. THE FIRST DOCTOR I SAW WASN'T VERY HELPFUL. IN FACT, HE COULDN'T CONCEIVE WHY I WOULD WANT TO EAT ONLY PLANT-BASED PROTEIN AND FELT HE COULDN'T DO ANYTHING TO HELP ME UNLESS I AGREED TO INCLUDE MEAT IN MY DIET. (WHICH, OF COURSE, I DIDN'T DO!)

Growing up I had a host of health problems. I struggled with my weight, had severe acne, dramatic mood swings, chronic digestive problems, and recurring bouts of pneumonia. One of these bouts even landed me in the emergency room. My mother was desperate to cure me and took me to all types of doctors—lung specialists, homeopaths, spirit doctors—you name it. At the same time, she was making sure I drank plenty of cow's milk, which she thought was good for me. Unfortunately, in my opinion, the milk was contributing to my lung problems and pneumonia.

When I was seventeen, I met a wonderful man who changed my life, Dr. José Efrain Melara. Dr. Melara was an eighty-six-year-old naturopathic doctor from El Salvador who could be mistaken for fifty. His practice was based on the fundamentals of naturopathy, an alternative medicine practice that favors a holistic approach to treatment with non-invasive techniques. His advice made perfect sense to me: follow a plant-based diet, learn to breathe correctly, get lots of exercise, and sleep well. After my first visit to Dr. Melara, I did a three-day cleansing juice diet. After those three days, it was as if I was a new person—my skin was glowing, I had so much more energy, and I had a great attitude and a feeling of renewal. Healthwise, I felt I was on the right track for the first time in my life.

My belief in the practice of both naturopathy and eating a plant-based diet is rooted in my thoughts about the evolution of human health. The gradual erosion of our diet has had a tremendously negative impact on our health as a society. Processed foods, dairy, refined sugars, and poor-quality food are making us sick. And instead of treating the source of the problem and changing our lifestyles to prevent the onset of illness, we seem to be satisfied by treating the symptoms with prescription after prescription in order to make life more manageable. Over the course of millions of years the human race has reached superior stages of intelligence and civilization. Unfortunately, the modern diet that most of us have adopted is literally killing us.

When I was twenty-three I lost the person in this world that I loved most, my dad. My father had major health problems: diabetes, high blood pressure, cardiovascular issues, and hepatitis. He'd experienced several strokes over the years; the last one took his life at the age of fifty-four. Whenever I tried to talk to him about his poor diet and lifestyle, he would laugh and say, "Are you planning to go to Mars with your flying saucer anytime soon?" He loved to enjoy life but had no interest in changing a lifetime of bad habits, which included a diet rich in red meat and other animal products. At the end he was lying in a hospital bed hooked up to a bunch of tubes, at the mercy of the machinery of modern medicine.

Eating a vegan diet has changed my life and radically improved my health. I have spent the past twenty years researching the best foods to eat—and the most delicious ways to prepare them. It is in the memory of my father that I hope to share this knowledge with the world so that more people will take steps to improve their own health.

A VEGAN WITH A SWEET TOOTH

In 2004, I was working as a journalist and public relations specialist in Rio de Janeiro. Even though I had become a vegan, I still had a major sweet tooth and craved high-quality chocolate, which I had trouble finding in Rio. Luckily, a friend of mine had opened a branch of the well-known Payard pâtisserie and restaurant in São Paolo, and he kept me supplied with good chocolate. In fact, I loved Payard's chocolates so much that I opened a branch of the Payard pâtisserie myself in Rio. This was the beginning of my food career. It was a big change from working in public relations. All of a sudden I was dealing with food orders, waiters, and cooks—it was a new world for me. I rented a kitchen and started doing a lot of catering for events and parties. Brazilians really watch their figures (probably because we want to look good on the beach), so in addition to all the butter-heavy pastries I prepared, I began to experiment with healthier options, using local fruits and organic and dairy-free ingredients. The response was overwhelming, and the business took off!

In 2009, my life changed again when I sold my business in Rio and moved to New York City. I knew that in order to continue in the food business I needed to follow my instinct and do something that I was passionate about and really believed in—something that would affect people's eating habits on a larger scale. Eventually the Vegan Divas concept was born: My goal was to combine high-quality, wholesome ingredients, classic pastry technique, and an elegant presentation to create a line of vegan treats so delicious that even non-vegans would come back for more. Today, with a bustling café, a constant stream of catering orders, and a devoted and loyal clientele, I consider that goal accomplished. Our bakery is successful because we allow people to indulge their sweet tooth without guilt. And the recipes in this book will help you do the same!

THE ETHICAL DIVA

Let me start by saying this: Even though I love it when people choose to eat a plant-based diet, I believe everyone has the freedom to eat what they want. The same way I expect people to respect the way I eat, I must respect other people's food choices. For me veganism is not just reflected in my diet; it's a life choice. But everyone is on his or her own journey and we must appreciate that.

Food is much more than nourishment; it is a cultural and social event that brings us together for everything from birthday parties to family celebrations to business events. Food also creates unforgettable memories and emotions that are translated into flavors, tastes, aromas, and colors that are linked to memories of our childhood, favorite places, and loved ones. Over time we find ourselves almost addicted to certain flavors and textures, whether it's a succulent steak, crispy fried chicken, rich, cheesy pasta, creamy ice cream, or any of the other "palate pleasers" that we have come to associate with the pleasure of life. It is this concept of palate pleasers—and the traditions handed down to us by our families—that largely dictates the choices we make when it comes to food. To me, there are other important considerations: our health, the health of animals, and the health of our planet.

In my opinion, being vegan not only offers a healthier lifestyle; it also makes it easier to extend compassion toward all living creatures (human and animal). I believe that pain is pain, and suffering is suffering, whether the victim is human or beast. I believe in the laws of karma, and that all suffering is intertwined. It's clear to me that the less we desire meat, the more aware we are of the suffering of animals and others. When veganism is supported by spiritual practice, it makes us more sympathetic. Whether we realize it or not, what we choose to eat is fundamentally linked to our spiritual beliefs as well as environmental and global issues.

The environment is also a key consideration in the vegan lifestyle. Large-scale, industrial livestock production is not sustainable for the planet. In the United States alone, half of all the water used is for livestock production. Seventy percent of land used to grow food in North America is used for animal feed. By growing this food and passing it through an animal first, a lot of energy is lost. If we all ate meat every day, there just wouldn't be enough food to feed us all without supplementing with plant-based foods.

The ecological effects of animal grazing are widespread, and the elimination of grazing holds greater potential for benefiting biodiversity than any other single land-use measure. In Amazonia, South America, rain forests are being destroyed at an alarming rate in order to clear the land for cattle grazing. Ranching-induced deforestation is one of the main reasons for the loss of plant and animal species in that area as well. Raising animals for food also generates more greenhouse gases than all the cars and trucks in the world combined. It's hard to believe, but a single dairy cow produces the equivalent of more than 1.5 metric tons of carbon dioxide! It's obvious to me that we need to change our ways—and by this I mean lifestyle and diet—before we destroy ourselves along with the planet.

EAT OUT LIKE A DIVA

Despite the common notion that vegans have a highly restricted diet, the truth is that there are a wide variety of food options included in a plant-based diet. More and more vegan restaurants are becoming more popular every day, and most non-vegan restaurants these days have at least one vegan dish on their menu. I recommend that you stick to simple options when ordering at a non-vegan restaurant, like salads or grilled vegetables accompanied by healthy legumes and high-protein grains like lentils, beans, quinoa and brown rice. Of course, you should always ask the waiter if there are any animal products in a dish (restaurants tend to use butter in almost everything!).

That said, I believe that food is meant to be enjoyed and shared with friends and family. When you go out to eat, the most important thing should be the company you're with and the overall experience of the meal. So while I believe that you should be careful with your food choices, I also understand that it isn't always realistic to stick to a vegan diet 100 percent of the time. If you're at a restaurant with limited options, don't deprive yourself of a meal and go hungry. And if you're on vacation or visiting an incredible restaurant and you want to taste a bite of a special dish, go for it (this happens to me all the time when I dine out with my dear chef friends or visit my husband's homeland, France—where they don't seem to understand the word *vegan*). Food is meant to be enjoyed. If you're making better choices for your health, the welfare of animals, and the planet 99 percent of the time, you are still doing a great thing.

I also encourage you to entertain at home. Not only does that guarantee that you will be able to eat something on the menu, it's also a great opportunity to introduce friends and family to vegan dishes. You might be thinking, *How can I serve vegan food to non-vegans?* It's easy—just serve food that tastes good and people will love it. It's a great way to show your friends that being vegan doesn't necessarily mean that you only eat tofu, and that shifting to a plant-based diet is not only a smart decision, but a delicious one. I don't pressure my non-vegan friends to change their ways. I believe I can influence people more by introducing them to a variety of great-tasting vegan dishes than I ever could by lecturing them.

part one

STOCKING THE VEGAN
DIVA PANTRY

COOKING AND BAKING VEGAN DISHES IS EASIER THAN YOU MIGHT THINK, BUT THERE ARE SOME KEY PANTRY ESSENTIALS I RECOMMEND KEEPING ON HAND. MANY OF THE INGREDIENTS I USE (ESPECIALLY FOR BAKING) ARE ONES YOU PROBABLY ALREADY HAVE AT HOME; OTHERS MAY BE NEW TO YOU. I'VE DIVIDED THE VEGAN DIVA PANTRY INTO TWO LISTS: BASICS AND SPECIALTIES. YOU CAN EASILY COMPARE THE BASIC ITEMS WITH WHAT YOU ALREADY HAVE ON HAND AND THEN, DEPENDING ON THE RECIPES YOU'D LIKE TO MAKE, THINK ABOUT WHICH MORE SPECIALIZED ITEMS YOU MAY WISH TO BUY—THEY WILL BE WELL WORTH THE INVESTMENT TO CREATE THE INCREDIBLE TREATS IN THE PAGES TO COME!

DIVA PANTRY BASICS

Unbleached all-purpose flour. This is the flour most often used in my baked goods. Look for a high-quality brand, preferably organic, such as King Arthur or Bob's Red Mill.

Whole wheat flour. Milled from the whole wheat kernel, whole wheat flour imparts a pleasantly nutty flavor and a coarse texture to baked goods. It has more fiber, vitamins, and minerals than standard all-purpose flour. Store whole wheat flour in an airtight container in the refrigerator, as it turns rancid quickly.

White whole wheat flour. This is whole wheat flour made from an albino variety of wheat. It has a mild, slightly nutty flavor, without the bitterness of traditional whole wheat flour but with the same nutritional benefits.

Cake flour. Cake flour contains less gluten and is more refined than all-purpose flour. Cakes and baked goods made with this flour will have a delicate grain and texture.

Flax seed meal. Flax seed meal is a great source of fiber, LNA (alpha-linoleic acid, which helps to reduce blood pressure, among other benefits), potassium, and magnesium, and can also be used as an egg substitute. Because it goes rancid quickly, I suggest you buy whole flax seeds, either brown or golden, and grind them in a coffee grinder as you need them. Store the seeds in an airtight container in the refrigerator or freezer.

Agave nectar. A natural sweetener, agave nectar is derived from the agave cactus and is about one and a half times sweeter than honey, with a more fluid consistency (closer to that of maple syrup). Agave nectar has a delicate flavor and can be used as a substitute for ingredients such as honey, maple syrup, and corn syrup.

Vegan Confectioners' sugar. Some confectioners' sugar is refined with animal bone char–based charcoal, so make sure to buy a brand that is identified as vegan.

Canola oil. Derived from rapeseeds, canola oil is very low in saturated fat and contains more monounsaturated fat than most oils (with the exception of olive oil). Canola oil also contains omega-3 fatty acids, which lower cholesterol and triglycerides.

Nonstick cooking spray. I use this convenient spray to prepare pans before baking. I prefer Original PAM organic brand, which is made from canola oil.

Baking powder. Make sure to use a baking powder that is aluminum-free, such as Rumford brand.

Coconut milk. This liquid comes from grated coconut meat and is available in full-fat and lite varieties. It is sold in cans—the "cream" and milk separate in the can, so make sure you give it a strong stir before using. Coconut milk is a good substitute for cow's milk in many recipes, but it does impart a strong coconut flavor, so take this into consideration. You can also chill a can of full-fat coconut milk, scoop off the hardened coconut cream, and whip it into a luscious topping for desserts (see page 197).

Rice milk. Rice milk is made by pressing rice through a mill and straining out the pressed grains. It is thinner than soy and cow's milk. Since boxed varieties don't require refrigeration until you open them, rice milk is a great pantry staple.

Cocoa powder. I use organic unsweetened natural cocoa powder—not alkalized or Dutch-processed cocoa—for all my recipes that call for cocoa powder. Natural cocoa powder has a more intense flavor than Dutch-processed and is more acidic, so it will react with baking soda in a recipe.

DIVA PANTRY SPECIALTIES

Brown rice flour. Made from unhulled rice kernels that have been finely ground, brown rice flour is gluten-free, and can be used as a partial substitute for wheat flour in many recipes.

Coconut flour. This gluten-free flour is made from coconut meat that is dried, defatted, and then finely ground. It contains a high percentage of dietary fiber (58 percent), which is another reason why I love it.

Organic whole wheat spelt flour. Spelt is a grain in the wheat family that has been cultivated for centuries in Europe and the Middle East. Its appearance is similar to wheat, and it does contain a moderate amount of gluten, but the gluten in spelt flour breaks down easily. Though spelt flour is not suitable for people with celiac disease, it is easy to digest, and many people who are sensitive to wheat can tolerate spelt.

Unleavened gluten-free baking flour. I use Bob's Red Mill Gluten-Free All-Purpose Flour for a few recipes in this book. It is made from a combination of garbanzo bean flour, potato starch, tapioca flour, white sorghum flour, and fava bean flour, and is great for baking gluten-free cookies, cakes, and muffins.

Agar agar. This odorless and tasteless seaweed derivative is a good vegan substitute for gelatin. It is available as a powder or as flakes.

Arrowroot. Arrowroot is a starch made from the roots of several tropical plants. It is an excellent thickener and has a neutral flavor. It can also be used as a substitute for wheat flour, as it's gluten-free, though it does not contain protein.

Potato starch. Potato starch is a thickener and can also be used to make cakes and other baked goods tender.

Tapioca starch. Made from ground cassava root, tapioca starch is an important ingredient in gluten-free baking. It adds structure to muffins and cookies without creating a gritty texture.

Brown rice syrup. About half as sweet as sugar, this amber-colored syrup is derived from fermented brown rice. To substitute it for sugar, use 1¼ cups brown rice syrup for each cup of sugar and use ¼ cup less of another liquid in the recipe.

Evaporated cane juice sugar. This unrefined cane sugar is made by dehydrating pressed cane juice and can be used in place of granulated sugar in recipes. Look for an organic brand that does not use any animal products in processing (some brands use bone char as a whitening agent). I recommend Florida Crystals brand.

Maple syrup. Made from the sap of sugar maple, black maple, or red maple trees, maple syrup is available in different grades. The most common grades used in baking are Dark Amber and Grade B, which are stronger in flavor than Grade A. Maple syrup adds a distinct flavor to recipes, so bear this in mind when substituting it for honey or other syrups.

Organic coconut palm sugar. This sugar comes from the sweet sap of the coconut palm tree flower, not the coconut fruit, so it does not have the flavor of coconut. I love it because it has a lower glycemic index (35) than agave (42) or cane sugar (68). It's also loaded with minerals such as potassium, magnesium, zinc, and iron and B vitamins. It has a deep caramel flavor and is a perfect replacement for refined brown sugar in oatmeal, coffee and other beverages, and in your recipes for baking.

Turbinado sugar. Also known as raw cane sugar, turbinado sugar is made from evaporated sugar cane juice that is centrifuged to produce large golden crystals. I love to sprinkle it onto cookies and piecrust just before baking to add color and crunch to the finished product.

Sucanat. This brand of sweetener (which stands for "sugar cane natural") is made by crushing sugar cane, extracting the juice, and heating it to a dark syrup. As the syrup cools, it is mixed with a paddle and eventually forms small brown crystals that have a mellow flavor. A bonus is that Sucanat retains molasses with its vitamins and minerals that are displaced by the processing of traditional brown sugar.

Almond oil. Made by pressing sweet almonds, almond oil has a delicate, nutty flavor that is ideal for flavoring salad dressings and baked goods.

Coconut oil and butter. Because it is high in saturated fat, coconut oil is solid at room temperature and is very stable, so it can be stored for a long time. I use this excellent fat frequently because it has a host of health benefits, including being great for your skin (in fact, I apply coconut butter all over my body and face to moisturize in the winter!). Nutiva coconut oil is 100 percent organic and extra-virgin. I use Artisana brand coconut butter—the company also makes almond, cashew, macadamia, walnut, and pecan butters. Note: Coconut oil is just the oil that is extracted from the meat. Coconut butter is the whole meat of the coconut pureed into a creamy butter. Coconut meat is approximately 65 percent oil.

Pumpkin seed oil. Made from pressed roasted pumpkin seeds, this greenish oil has an intensely nutty flavor and is rich in polyunsaturated fatty acids. It can be used as a flavor accent in anything from salad dressings to desserts.

Walnut oil. Made from pressed walnuts, this light-colored oil has a delicate, nutty flavor and scent. It is a good source of omega-3 fatty acids, and is best used in salad dressings and to add flavor to desserts and baked goods.

Egg replacer. I use a powdered egg replacer called Ener-G Egg Replacer, which is gluten-free. Mix 1½ teaspoons dry egg replacer with 2 tablespoons water to replace each egg called for in a recipe.

Non-dairy chocolate morsels. Look for high-quality chocolate morsels that are dairy-free and labeled "vegan." I like Sunspire brand, which is available at Whole Foods and many other grocery stores.

Vegan Bittersweet Chocolate. Bittersweet chocolate is used in many of my chocolate recipes, like the Chocolate Brownie Mousse Parfait (page 118) and my Chocolate Liégeois with Tofu-Tahini Ice Cream (page 120). I like the Sunspire brand bittersweet chocolate.

Kombu. Made from dried sea kelp, kombu is used in Japanese cooking and is a main ingredient in dashi, a stock that is the base for many soups.

Nutritional yeast. Because of its distinctive "cheesy" flavor, nutritional yeast flakes are frequently used as a seasoning in vegan cooking. I use them to flavor my delicious Kale Chips (page 173).

THE DIVA FRIDGE

Almond milk. Made from ground almonds and water, almond milk is a good substitute for cow's milk in most recipes.

Miso. This thick, fermented soy paste is high in protein, vitamins, and minerals and is frequently used to add flavor to soups and salad dressings.

Soy creamer. Soy creamer comes in small cartons, just like regular dairy creamer, and is available in the dairy section of most grocery stores. Make sure to select an unflavored variety for baking—I use soy creamer in several recipes in this book, including my Pumpkin Scones (page 36) and Espresso-Lemon Panna Cotta (page 112). Use any leftover creamer in your coffee or tea—it's delicious!

Soy milk. Made from soybeans that have been soaked in water, soy milk is available in fat-free varieties and a multitude of flavors—though you will want to use unflavored soy milk in most baked goods. Always try to purchase organic soy milk, as many soy crops are heavily treated with pesticides. Some varieties are made with genetically modified soy beans. Look for "non-GMO" on the label.

Soy yogurt. This is yogurt made from soy milk, and it contains less fat than yogurt made with cow's milk.

Tempeh. Tempeh is made from cooked and fermented soybeans that are formed into a cake. It has an earthy, nutty flavor and is frequently eaten as a meat substitute. It is sold plain or smoked and in a variety of flavors, such as lemon pepper or coconut curry. Tempeh is high in protein, fiber, and vitamins.

Tofu. Made by pressing soy curds into blocks, tofu is available fresh or processed and in a variety of textures, depending on the amount of water that has been pressed out. It has a very subtle flavor and can be used as an egg substitute in baked goods. Tofu is low in calories and fat and is a good source of protein and iron, which makes it a great addition to salads and vegetable dishes. As with other soy products, look for "non-GMO" on the label.

Tofu water. This is the water drained from a package of tofu. I pour it into a covered container and store it in the refrigerator to use in recipes as a thickening agent. It will keep for up to a week.

Vegan butter. Non-dairy and non-hydrogenated, this butter substitute is made from a blend of vegetable oils. I recommend Earth Balance Vegan Buttery Sticks, which are made with a blend of palm fruit, canola, soybean, flax, and olive oils and soy protein.

Vegan butter spread. I use Earth Balance brand, a non-hydrogenated spread that is made from a proprietary blend of vegetable oils and is formulated to be slightly lighter and more spreadable than vegan butter sticks.

Vegan cream cheese. When I use vegan cream cheese, I use Tofutti Better Than Cream Cheese, which tastes very close to dairy cream cheese, but with less of a tang. Make sure that whatever kind you choose is free of hydrogenated oils.

Vegan shortening. Look for a non-hydrogenated vegetable shortening such as Earth Balance or Spectrum brand, which are made from 100 percent palm oil.

THE WELL-EQUIPPED DIVA

Here's a list of the kitchen equipment that will make your vegan baking and cooking experiences successful and *that much* easier.

Baking pans. You'll need the following sizes: 8- and 9-inch square pans; 9-by-13-inch pan; 9-inch deep-dish pie pan; 9-by-5-inch and 8-by-4-inch loaf pans; and 9½-inch springform pan.

Baking sheets. You should have three or four heavy-gauge stainless steel* baking sheets, also known as half sheet pans, in your collection. Each measures 17½ by 11½ inches.

Bread machine. This optional piece of equipment takes the hassle out of bread making. So much so, in fact, you may never buy bread again. You'll need a bread machine to make Nanda's Cinnamon Buns (page 138).

Cookie scoops. I love to use these small scoops to portion out perfect mounds of cookie dough. My favorite size for cookies is a 1½-ounce scoop, though you may want to have a few sizes on hand.

Digital kitchen scale. This is one of the most important tools to ensure your baking success, as measuring ingredients by weight is much more accurate

---

* Note: I recommend stainless steel, because aluminum is bad for our health as it has been linked to diseases such as epilepsy, dementia, osteomalacia, ADD, and chronic fatigue syndrome. It has also been linked to Alzheimer's disease. Always avoid using aluminum pans in the kitchen, and never wrap food in aluminum foil.

than measuring by volume. You'll notice that in each of my recipes I offer alternative metric measurements in weight only, not volume.

Food processor. I use my food processor all the time for a variety of tasks, including chopping nuts, pureeing soups, making pie dough, and blending batters.

Heavy-duty electric stand mixer with paddle and whisk attachments. Once you start using an electric stand mixer, you'll wonder how you ever got along without one. I recommend the KitchenAid brand mixer, which will last forever.

Measuring cups and spoons. Have a set of good-quality graduated dry measuring cups on hand, as well as a set of measuring spoons.

Microplane zester. I use this fantastic tool for a variety of tasks in the kitchen, including removing zest from citrus fruits, finely grating vegan chocolate, and shaving nuts.

Mixing bowls. Have stainless steel bowls in a variety of sizes on hand.

Muffins pans. A standard 12-cup muffin pan is used for making all the muffin recipes in this book.

Oven thermometer. An accurate oven thermometer is essential to ensure that your baked goods will not be overcooked or undercooked. As oven thermostats are often inaccurate, I recommend using an oven thermometer every time you bake.

Pastry blender. This simple little tool is indispensable for cutting vegan butter and shortening into flour to make scones, biscuits, and pie dough.

Pastry brushes. You will need a good-quality 1½-inch pastry brush (either with bristles or silicone) for oiling pans and brushing dough.

Pastry cutters. It's helpful to have a set of nested round pastry cutters in graduated sizes for cutting biscuits and rolled cookies.

Rolling pin. You'll need a good wooden rolling pin for rolling out pie and cookie doughs. My preference is for the simple dowel-style pin, but you may prefer the heavier ball-bearing rolling pins with handles.

Rubber spatulas. These are essential for folding ingredients together and scraping the last bits of batter and dough out of bowls. Have a few small and large ones on hand.

Sieve. A fine-mesh sieve can be used to sift dry ingredients and is indispensable for straining sauces and fillings.

Silicone baking mats or parchment paper. You will need either a few silicone baking mats or a supply of parchment paper for lining baking sheets to prevent cookies and other baked goods from sticking.

Small and large metal offset spatulas. These tools are great for spreading out batters and frosting cakes and cupcakes.

Small electric spice or coffee grinder. A small electric grinder is useful for grinding flax seeds and spices.

Stainless steel dough scraper. This rectangular metal device has a wooden handle on one edge and is used for cutting and portioning yeast doughs, transferring chopped nuts and other ingredients, and cleaning off counter-tops and cutting boards.

Timer. A reliable timer is crucial for baking. Get a digital one that you can hang around your neck so that you're not chained to the kitchen!

Vegetable peeler. You will use this a lot if you're following a vegan diet! My favorite is the Oxo vegetable peeler.

Whipped cream canister. This gadget, which uses a nitrous oxide charger to aerate ingredients, is really handy for making vegan whipped topping and soy milk foam to top desserts. The brand ISI makes the version that most chefs use.

Whisks. Have a few sizes on hand for whisking lump-free sauces and icings.

Wire cooling racks. Wire racks are used to support baked goods like cookies and layer cakes so that they cool properly after baking. Have at least two sturdy wire racks on hand.

part two

LET'S DO
BRUNCH

GLUTEN-FREE ORANGE ALMOND COCONUT MUFFINS

A combination of brown rice flour, almond flour, and arrowroot replaces wheat flour in these delicious gluten-free muffins. The flavors of orange, coconut, and almond blend nicely here, with maple syrup adding a subtle back note of sweetness. Serve these for breakfast, brunch, or an afternoon snack.

MAKES 10 MUFFINS

1 cup (177 g/6.25 oz) brown rice flour
2/3 cup (58 g/2 oz) almond flour
1/2 cup (70 g/2.46 oz) arrowroot
1/3 cup (56 g/2 oz) Sucanat
2 teaspoons (10 g/0.34 oz) baking powder
1/2 teaspoon (1.5 g/0.05 oz) kosher salt
1/3 cup (100 g/3.5 oz) maple syrup
1/2 cup (121 g/4.3 oz) orange juice
Finely grated zest of 1 orange
1 1/2 teaspoons (6 g/0.21 oz) vanilla extract
1/2 cup (42 g/1.5 oz) chopped almonds
1/4 cup (21 g/0.75 oz) unsweetened shredded coconut

Preheat the oven to 375°F. Line 10 cups in a 12-cup muffin pan with paper liners, or grease them well with coconut oil.

In a large bowl, mix together the brown rice flour, almond flour, arrowroot, Sucanat, baking powder, and salt. Make a well in the center, then add the maple syrup, orange juice, orange zest, and vanilla. Gradually stir the dry ingredients into the wet ones, mixing just until blended. Stir in the almonds and coconut.

Spoon the batter into the prepared cups, filling them two-thirds full, and smooth the top of each muffin. Bake for 12 to 16 minutes, until a toothpick inserted into the center of the muffins comes out clean. Cool the muffins in the pan set on a wire rack for at least 15 minutes before serving.

The Savvy Diva

Because brown rice flour contains natural oils that can oxidize and turn rancid quickly, always store it in a sealed plastic bag in the refrigerator or freezer.

TOFU YOGURT MY WAY

Non-dairy soy yogurt is relatively easy to find in supermarkets nowadays, but it's also super-easy to make your own at home (and a *lot* less expensive than buying it!). Here's my basic recipe, but feel free to flavor yours with your favorite fruit or sweeten it with agave or maple syrup. I love to serve mine in a beautiful glass as a parfait, layered with fresh berries and my Detox Granola. What better way to start the day?

MAKES TWO 1-CUP (225 G/8 OZ) SERVINGS

One 12.3-ounce (349-g) package tofu, any firmness
1 medium (118 g/4.16 oz) ripe, cold banana, sliced
2 tablespoons (30 g/1 oz) almond milk
2 tablespoons (30 g/1 oz) fresh lemon juice
1/2 teaspoon (2.5 g/0.08 oz) vanilla extract
1/4 cup Detox Granola (page 32), for serving
Fresh berries (optional)

In the bowl of a food processor, combine the tofu, banana slices, almond milk, lemon juice, and vanilla and process until smooth and creamy, about 1 minute. Divide between 2 parfait glasses or bowls and serve with granola or fresh berries. The yogurt can be stored in an airtight container in the refrigerator for up to 3 days.

Tofu Yogurt My Way with Detox Granola

DETOX GRANOLA

One of the most popular items at Vegan Divas, our all-natural Detox Granola is not just for the tree-hugging set—everybody loves it, and for good reason. It's full of a variety of amazing ingredients—whole grain oats, flax, coconut, spices, and a medley of dried fruit, all sweetened with a touch of maple syrup and soft-baked to crunchy perfection. It's a great thing to wake up to, but you might find yourself eating it just about anytime!

MAKES ABOUT 7 CUPS (740 G/26 OZ)

2 cups (222 g/7.8 oz) rolled oats

1/2 cup (60 g/2.1 oz) sliced almonds

1/4 cup (28 g/1 oz) chopped walnuts

1/4 cup (28 g/1 oz) chopped Brazil nuts

1/4 cup (22 g/0.8 oz) unsweetened desiccated coconut

1/4 cup (42 g/1.5 oz) ground golden flax seed meal (see Vegan Ingredient Sources, page 205)

1/4 teaspoon (0.75 g/0.026 oz) kosher salt

1/4 teaspoon (0.5 g/0.01 oz) ground cinnamon

1/8 teaspoon (0.25 g/0.009 oz) ground cloves

1/8 teaspoon (0.25 g/0.009 oz) freshly grated nutmeg

1/4 cup (75 g/2.6 oz) maple syrup

1 1/2 tablespoons (15 g/0.5 oz) liquid coconut oil

1/2 cup (50 g/1.76 oz) dried apples, chopped

1/4 cup (40 g/1.4 oz) dried cherries

1/2 cup (80 g/2.8 oz) dried cranberries

1/2 cup (80 g/2.8 oz) raisins

1/4 cup (40 g/1.4 oz) chopped dried apricots

1/4 cup (40 g/1.4 oz) chopped dried figs

Preheat the oven to 325°F. Line a large rimmed baking sheet with parchment paper or a silicone baking mat. Generously coat the sides of the pan with nonstick cooking spray and set aside.

In a large bowl, combine the oats, nuts, coconut, flax seed meal, salt, and spices. Mix together well with your hands.

In a medium bowl, whisk together the maple syrup and coconut oil until blended. Pour the mixture over the oat mixture and mix together with your hands until the dry mixture is completely coated. Evenly distribute the granola on the prepared baking sheet. Bake for 15 to 20 minutes, until crisp and golden brown, tossing the granola 3 times during baking to ensure even browning. Cool completely.

Stir the dried fruit into the granola and store in an airtight container at room temperature for up to a month.

PEANUT BUTTER AND JELLY SCONES

Peanut butter and jelly just may be the most comforting combination of flavors known to mankind. In place of jelly, I use a good organic raspberry jam in these tender scones and swirl it through the dough so that you get little bursts of jam in every bite. Rewarm them in a 325°F oven for 5 minutes before serving for maximum gooiness.

MAKES 8 SCONES

1 cup (128 g/4.5 oz) unbleached all-purpose flour

2 teaspoons (10 g/0.35 oz) baking powder

1/4 cup (40 g/1.4 oz) turbinado sugar, plus extra to sprinkle on top

1/4 teaspoon (0.75 g/0.026 oz) kosher salt

3 tablespoons (36 g/1.3 oz) vegan shortening

1/4 cup plus 2 1/2 tablespoons (90 g/3.17 oz) soy milk

3/4 teaspoon (3.7 g/0.13 oz) apple cider vinegar

2 teaspoons (6.6 g/0.23 oz) liquid coconut oil

1/4 teaspoon (1.2 g/0.04 oz) vanilla extract

3 tablespoons (45 g/1.6 oz) smooth peanut butter

1 tablespoon plus 1 teaspoon (20 g/0.7 oz) organic raspberry jam

Preheat the oven to 325°F. Line a baking sheet with parchment paper or a silicone baking mat.

In a medium bowl, whisk together the flour, baking powder, sugar, and salt until combined. Add the shortening to the mixture and, using your hands, mix until crumbly. Make a well in the center of the mixture. Add the soy milk, vinegar, oil, vanilla, peanut butter, and jam to the well and gradually mix together the liquids into the dry ingredients.

Half fill a small (1 1/2-ounce) ice cream scoop (or fill a 1/4 measuring cup about three-quarters full) with the batter, then top with 1 teaspoon of the raspberry jam. Fill the scoop with more batter, then swirl the jam through the batter in the scoop with the tip of a knife. Release the scoop of batter onto the prepared pan. Repeat with the remaining batter, spacing the scones 3 inches apart.

Sprinkle each scone with turbinado sugar and bake for 12 to 15 minutes, until the scones are golden and their centers are firm. Serve the scones warm with a dollop of extra raspberry jam on top.

Store the scones in an airtight container at room temperature for up to 3 days or in the refrigerator for up to a week.

PUMPKIN SCONES

I love to make these delicious double-glazed pumpkin scones throughout the fall season, though there's no reason why you can't enjoy them year-round. Tender scones can be tricky to achieve—work the dough too much and they can turn into hockey pucks. For the best results, treat the dough gently as you're gathering it together, only kneading it softly a few times if necessary.

MAKES 6 LARGE SCONES

SCONES:
2 cups (250 g/8.8 oz) whole wheat flour
1/4 cup (50 g/1.75 oz) evaporated cane juice sugar
1 tablespoon (15 g/0.5 oz) baking powder
1/2 teaspoon (1 g/0.035 oz) ground cinnamon
1/2 teaspoon (1 g/0.035 oz) ground nutmeg
1/4 teaspoon (0.5 g/0.017 oz) ground ginger
1/4 teaspoon (0.75 g/0.025 oz) kosher salt
4 tablespoons (56 g/2 oz) vegan butter, cut into 1/2-inch pieces
1/2 cup (120 g/4.2 oz) canned pumpkin puree (not pumpkin pie filling)
1/3 cup (77 g/2.7 oz) soy creamer

GLAZE:
1 cup (114 g/4 oz) vegan confectioners' sugar, sifted
2 tablespoons (37 g/1.3 oz) maple syrup
1 to 2 tablespoons (14 to 28 g/0.5 to 1 oz) soy creamer

DRIZZLE:
1 cup (114 g/4 oz) vegan confectioners' sugar
2 tablespoons (28 g/1 oz) soy creamer
1/4 teaspoon (0.5 g/0.02 oz) ground cinnamon
Pinch of ground ginger
Pinch of freshly grated nutmeg

Preheat the oven to 425°F. Line a baking sheet with parchment paper or a silicone baking mat.

MAKE THE SCONES:

In a large bowl, whisk together the flour, sugar, baking powder, spices, and salt. Scatter the butter over the mixture and, using a pastry blender or 2 knives, cut it into the dry ingredients until the largest pieces are the size of peas and the rest resembles coarse meal.

In another large bowl, whisk together the pumpkin puree and soy creamer. Stir this mixture gently into the flour mixture just until the dough comes together (you may have to knead it very gently a few times).

Scrape the dough onto a lightly floured work surface and lightly dust it with more flour. Shape it into a 9-inch disc (use a rolling pin to lightly roll the dough if necessary, but the scones will be more tender if you pat it out with your hands). Cut the disc in half, then cut each half into 3 wedges for a total of 6 wedges. Transfer the wedges to the baking sheet, spacing them 2 inches apart. Bake for 15 to 18 minutes, until golden around the edges. Transfer the scones to a baking rack with a piece of parchment paper underneath and cool while you make the glaze.

MAKE THE GLAZE:

Whisk together vegan confectioners' sugar, maple syrup, and soy creamer in a medium bowl until smooth. Spread about 1 tablespoon of the glaze over each warm scone.

MAKE THE DRIZZLE:

Whisk together vegan confectioners' sugar, soy creamer, cinnamon, ginger, and nutmeg in another medium bowl until smooth. When the scones have cooled, drizzle the mixture over the scones with a fork.

Store the scones in an airtight container at room temperature for up to 3 days or in the refrigerator for up to a week. For best results, warm them up for 5 minutes in an oven preheated to 325°F before serving.

EGGLESS SCRAMBLED EGGS

This dish may look uncannily like scrambled eggs, but tofu is the main ingredient here. Turmeric gives it a bright yellow hue and earthy flavor, while caramelized onions, kale, tomato, and basil make it a hearty dish that's ideal for Sunday brunch. If you don't have kale on hand, feel free to substitute whatever vegetables are in your fridge. I like to use nonstick ceramic pans (see page 204) when cooking eggs—they are safer than coated nonstick pans.

SERVES 2

Half 14-ounce package (200 g/7 oz) extra-firm silken tofu
2 tablespoons (28 g/1 oz) olive oil
1 medium onion, finely chopped
1 teaspoon (2 g/0.07 oz) ground turmeric
1 medium tomato, cored and chopped
2 medium leaves kale, shredded
2 tablespoons (5 g/0.176 oz) chopped fresh basil leaves
Sea salt and freshly ground black pepper
Dash of Tabasco sauce
Avocado and tomato slices for garnish

Drain the tofu and gently pat it dry with a paper towel. Place the tofu in a bowl and, using a fork, break it up into large (about 1/2-inch) "crumbs." Set aside.

Heat the olive oil in a large nonstick skillet over medium heat. Add the onion, reduce the heat to medium-low, and cook, stirring occasionally, until the onion turns golden brown and caramelizes, about 25 minutes. Add the crumbled tofu and turmeric and cook, stirring, for 2 minutes. Add the chopped tomato, kale, and basil and cook for 3 minutes longer. Season with salt and pepper and add the Tabasco. Serve immediately, garnished with avocado and tomato slices.

The Savvy Diva

The health benefits of turmeric, a yellow spice used frequently in Indian cooking, are numerous. Turmeric has anti-inflammatory and antioxidant properties that aid in the prevention of various types of cancer, arthritis, and Alzheimer's disease. Turmeric has also been shown to lower cholesterol.

PERFECT PANCAKES

Vegans and non-vegans alike will love these light, fluffy pancakes. If you want to boost their nutritional value, add some golden flax seeds—a good source of fiber and omega-3s—to the batter before cooking. Serve with warm maple syrup, fresh berries, and a selection of jams.

MAKES ABOUT EIGHT 5-INCH PANCAKES

1 cup (128 g/4.5 oz) unbleached all-purpose flour
2 teaspoons (10 g/0.35 oz) baking powder
1/2 teaspoon (1.5 g/0.05 oz) kosher salt
2 tablespoons (25 g/0.88 oz) evaporated cane juice sugar
1 1/2 teaspoons (6 g/0.21 oz) egg replacer mixed with
    2 tablespoons (30 g/1 oz) warm water
1 cup (242 g/8.5 oz) soy milk
2 tablespoons (28 g/1 oz) sunflower oil

In a large bowl, whisk together the flour, baking powder, salt, and sugar; set aside.

In a medium bowl, whisk together the egg replacer mixture, soy milk, and oil, then gently whisk it into the dry ingredients until just combined (the batter should be somewhat lumpy).

Preheat a griddle or large skillet and coat it with nonstick cooking spray. Pour about 1/3 cup batter onto the hot griddle for each pancake and cook until the top of each pancake is speckled with bubbles, then turn over and cook on the other side for 30 to 60 seconds, until lightly browned. Serve immediately or keep the pancakes warm in a preheated 300°F oven.

SWEET POTATO PANCAKES

These delicious pancakes are surprisingly light, with a moist interior and slightly crisp exterior. Because they are made with sweet potatoes, they are denser than traditional pancakes and take a little longer to cook. Sweet potatoes are an excellent source of vitamins C, E, and B_{12}, calcium, potassium, magnesium, and fiber, so you can absolutely feel guilt-free eating these for brunch. Serve with warm maple syrup, fresh fruit, and Eggless Scrambled Eggs (page 39).

MAKES 15 PANCAKES

2 teaspoons (10 g/0.35 oz) apple cider vinegar

3 cups (726 g/25.6 oz) soy milk

1 cup (125 g/4.4 oz) whole wheat flour

3/4 cup (96 g/3.3 oz) unbleached all-purpose flour

2 tablespoons (25 g/0.88 oz) evaporated cane juice sugar

2 teaspoons (10 g/0.35 oz) baking powder

1/2 teaspoon (2.5 g/0.09 oz) baking soda

1/4 teaspoon (0.75 g/0.03 oz) kosher salt

51/3 tablespoons (75 g/2.6 oz) cold vegan butter, cut into 1/2-inch cubes

11/2 cups (340 g/12 oz) cooked and mashed sweet potatoes

Stir the vinegar into the soy milk and set aside for 10 minutes to curdle (this will make soy "buttermilk").

In a large bowl, combine the flours, sugar, baking powder, baking soda, and salt. Add the butter cubes and, using a pastry blender or 2 knives, cut it into the mixture until it resembles coarse crumbs (you can also do this in a food processor). Stir in the curdled soy milk until blended. Add the sweet potato puree and mix until combined (the mixture will be lumpy).

Preheat a griddle or large skillet over medium heat and coat it with nonstick cooking spray. Pour about 1/3 cup batter onto the hot griddle for each pancake and cook until the top of each is speckled with bubbles (these pancakes take a little longer to cook than traditional ones, and the cooking time will vary depending on your griddle or stove), about 2 minutes, then turn over and cook on the other side for another minute, or until lightly browned. Serve immediately or keep the pancakes warm in a 300°F oven.

SAVORY OLIVE AND ROSEMARY SCONES

These savory scones are flavored with woodsy rosemary and bits of chopped olive and are best eaten warm, straight from the oven. If olives are not your thing, feel free to substitute scallions, chives, or chopped sun-dried tomatoes in their place. Serve these scones for brunch, tea, or anytime you want a hearty snack.

MAKES 8 SCONES

1 cup (128 g/4.5 oz) unbleached all-purpose flour

2 teaspoons (10 g/0.35 oz) baking powder

$1/8$ teaspoon (0.6 g/0.02 oz) baking soda

$1/4$ teaspoon (0.75 g/0.026 oz) kosher salt

2 tablespoons plus $1^1/_2$ teaspoons (32 g/1.12 oz) vegan shortening

$1/4$ cup plus $2^1/_2$ tablespoons (97 g/3.4 oz) soy milk

$3/4$ teaspoon (3.75 g/0.13 oz) apple cider vinegar

2 teaspoons (9 g/0.3 oz) liquid coconut oil

$1/4$ cup to $1/3$ cup (45 g to 60 g/1.6 oz to 2.1 oz) chopped
   pitted black or green olives

2 teaspoons (3 g/0.1 oz) chopped rosemary leaves

Preheat the oven to 325°F. Line a large baking sheet with parchment paper or a silicone baking mat.

In a medium bowl, gently whisk together the flour, baking powder, baking soda, and salt until combined. Add the shortening to the mixture and, using your fingers, mix it in until it is evenly distributed and the mixture is crumbly. Make a well in the center of the mixture. Add the soy milk, vinegar, oil, chopped olives, and rosemary to the well and gradually mix them into the dry ingredients with a rubber spatula until just blended. Using a $1^1/_2$-ounce ice cream scoop, scoop out 8 portions of the dough onto the prepared baking sheet, spacing them at least 2 inches apart. Bake for 12 to 15 minutes, until the scones are golden and their centers are firm.

THE SAVVY DIVA

To pit olives, I put them on a cutting board, place the flat side of a chef's knife on top, and give it a firm whack. This splits the olive open, exposing the pit and allowing it to be removed easily.

part three

AFTERNOON
PICK-ME-UPS

VEGAN DIVAS CHOCOLATE BROWNIES

These moist, fudgy brownies helped put our little bakery on the map—once people taste them they keep coming back for more: their dense, rich chocolate flavor will satisfy even the most ardent chocophile in search of a fix. For even more of a chocolate kick, add 1 cup vegan chocolate morsels to the batter.

MAKES 16 BROWNIES

2 cups (256 g/9 oz) unbleached all-purpose flour
2 cups (307 g/10.8 oz) Sucanat
3/4 cup (70 g/2.4 oz) unsweetened natural cocoa powder
1 teaspoon (5 g/0.17 oz) baking powder
1 teaspoon (3 g/0.1 oz) kosher salt
1 cup (236 g/8.3 oz) water
1 cup (160 g/5.6 oz) liquid coconut oil
1 teaspoon (4 g/0.14 oz) vanilla extract
Vegan confectioners' sugar, sifted, for garnsh

Preheat the oven to 350°F. Coat the bottom and sides of a 9-by-13-inch baking pan with nonstick cooking spray.

In a large bowl, stir together the flour, Sucanat, cocoa powder, baking powder, and salt. Make a well in the center of the dry ingredients, pour the water, coconut oil, and vanilla in, and mix just until blended. Spread the batter evenly into the prepared pan. Bake for 20 to 25 minutes, until the top is no longer shiny. Let cool in the pan on a wire rack for at least 30 minutes, then cut into sixteen 2$\frac{1}{2}$-by-3$\frac{1}{2}$-inch rectangles. Dust with the sifted confectioners' sugar.

MAPLE PECAN SABLE COOKIES

These melt-in-your-mouth cookies are flavored with maple syrup and toasted pecans. Nestled in a ribbon-wrapped tin, they make a wonderful gift, but you may find it difficult to give away these petite treats. Macadamia nuts make a nice substitute for the pecans— just reduce the oven temperature to 325°F for toasting them, as they are a bit more delicate. You can also substitute unleavened gluten-free baking flour for the spelt flour if you prefer a gluten-free cookie.

MAKES ABOUT 36 COOKIES

3/4 cup (85 g/3 oz) chopped pecans
1/2 cup (113 g/4 oz) vegan butter
1/4 cup (56 g/2 oz) light brown sugar
3 tablespoons (56 g/2 oz) maple syrup
1/2 teaspoon (2.5 g/0.09 oz) vanilla extract
1/2 teaspoon (1.5 g/0.05 oz) kosher salt
11/3 cups (177 g/6.2 oz) organic whole wheat spelt flour, plus extra for dusting
1/4 cup (40 g/1.4 oz) turbinado sugar for coating the cookies

Preheat the oven to 350°F.

Scatter the chopped pecans on a baking sheet and toast for 8 to 10 minutes, until lightly browned and fragrant. Cool completely.

In the bowl of an electric mixer using the paddle attachment, beat the butter with the brown sugar, maple syrup, vanilla, and salt at high speed until creamy, about 2 minutes, scraping down the sides of the bowl with a rubber spatula as necessary. Reduce the speed to low and add the flour, mixing just until blended. Add the pecans and mix until combined.

Lightly dust a work surface with some flour. Transfer the dough to the work surface and shape it into a 10-inch-long log (about 11/2 inches in diameter). Wrap the log in plastic wrap and refrigerate for 2 hours, or until firm.

Unwrap the dough log and let stand at room temperature for 20 minutes.

Position 2 racks near the center of the oven and preheat the oven to 350°F. Line 2 baking sheets with parchment paper or silicone mats.

Spread the turbinado sugar out onto a work surface and roll the log in it to lightly coat. Using a chef's knife, slice the log into 1/4-inch rounds and arrange them on the lined baking sheets, spacing them 2 inches apart. Bake the cookies for 12 to 14 minutes, swapping the position of the racks halfway through baking, until the cookies are golden around the edges. Cool the cookies on the pan on wire racks for 10 minutes. Transfer the cookies to the racks and cool completely.

HOST LIKE A DIVA

These pretty, delicate cookies are not only delicious; they also keep well, making them perfect for holiday gifts or parties. You can make several batches in advance and store them in a sealed container at room temperature for up to 3 weeks. They also freeze well—if sealed properly, they will keep in the freezer for several months.

COCONUT CHOCOLATE PECAN BARS

"Addictive" is the only way I can describe these gooey, rich dessert bars. Their pastry base is made from a combination of almond and spelt flour and is sweetened with maple syrup. The topping is made from a reduction of coconut milk and Sucanat, with coconut, pecans, and vegan chocolate morsels providing the chewy, melt-in-your-mouth goodness on top.

MAKES 24 BARS

ALMOND CRUST:
1³/₄ cups (165 g/5.8 oz) almond flour
¹/₃ cup (41 g/1.4 oz) organic whole wheat spelt flour
Pinch of kosher salt
¹/₃ cup (98 g/3.5 oz) maple syrup
¹/₃ cup (74 g/2.6 oz) liquid coconut oil

COCONUT FILLING:
One 14-ounce (397-g) can coconut milk (regular or lite)
²/₃ cup (102 g/3.6 oz) Sucanat
1 tablespoon (12 g/0.42 oz) vanilla extract
1¹/₂ cups (255 g/9 oz) vegan semisweet chocolate morsels
2 cups (180 g/6.3 oz) unsweetened desiccated coconut
1 cup (100 g/3.5 oz) pecans, chopped

MAKE THE CRUST:
Preheat the oven to 350°F. Coat the bottom and sides of a 9-by-13-inch baking pan with nonstick cooking spray.

Place the almond flour, spelt flour, and salt in a medium bowl and whisk to combine. Combine the maple syrup and coconut oil in a small bowl or glass measuring cup and fold the liquids into the flour mixture until blended. Press the almond mixture onto the bottom of the prepared pan, covering the bottom. Bake for 8 to 10 minutes, until lightly browned. Cool the crust in the pan on a wire rack while you make the filling. Leave the oven on.

MAKE THE FILLING:

Combine the coconut milk and Sucanat in a medium saucepan over medium heat and bring to a simmer. Reduce the heat to medium-low and simmer for about 10 minutes, whisking occasionally, until slightly thickened. Remove the pan from the heat and let the mixture cool for 5 minutes.

Stir the vanilla into the coconut milk mixture. Scatter the chocolate morsels over the crust, then top with the coconut and pecans. Slowly pour the coconut milk mixture on top. Bake the bars for 20 to 25 minutes, until golden brown and bubbly. Cool the bars completely in the pan set on a wire rack.

Refrigerate the bars for at least 3 hours or overnight, then cut into squares and serve.

THE SAVVY DIVA

Unsweetened desiccated coconut is different from regular shredded coconut. Desiccated coconut is shredded, dried, and then ground to a very fine flake. It is widely available online or at health food stores and many supermarkets.

EASY COFFEE CAKE

This exceptionally moist snack-cake is fragrant with apples and spices and will fill your kitchen with wonderful, warm aromas. I love to eat a square of this cake with a cup of tea in the afternoon, when my energy is lagging and I need a little pick-me-up.

SERVES 9

> 4 tablespoons (56 g/2 oz) vegan butter, cut into tablespoons
> 2 cups (484 g/17 oz) unsweetened applesauce
> 1 cup (128 g/4.5 oz) unbleached all-purpose flour
> 1½ cups (120 g/4.2 oz) rolled oats (not quick-cooking)
> 1 cup (200 g/7 oz) evaporated cane juice sugar
> 1 teaspoon (5 g/0.17 oz) baking soda
> 1 teaspoon (2 g/0.07 oz) ground cinnamon
> ½ teaspoon (1 g/0.035 oz) freshly grated nutmeg
> ¼ teaspoon (0.5 g/0.017 oz) ground cloves
> 1 cup (149 g/5.2 oz) black raisins

Coat the bottom and sides of a 9-inch square baking pan with nonstick cooking spray.

In a large saucepan, combine the butter and applesauce and heat over medium heat, stirring occasionally, until the butter is melted. Remove from the heat and set aside to cool for 15 minutes.

Preheat the oven to 350°F.   ·

Stir the remaining ingredients into the cooled applesauce mixture, mixing until well combined, then pour into the prepared baking pan. Bake the cake for 35 to 40 minutes, until a toothpick inserted into its center comes out clean. Cool in the pan on a wire rack.

Cut the cake into squares and serve with coffee or tea.

LEMON-ROSEMARY BUTTER COOKIES

The woodsy flavor of fresh rosemary pairs really well with lemon, especially in these tender cookies. Rolling them in the turbinado sugar before baking makes the cookies sparkle like the little jewels they are. I like to serve these with tea in the afternoon.

MAKES ABOUT 40 COOKIES

1/2 cup (113 g/4 oz) vegan butter, softened
1/4 cup (50 g/1.76 oz) evaporated cane juice sugar
1 teaspoon (3 g/0.1 oz) finely chopped fresh rosemary
1/2 teaspoon (1 g/0.03 oz) finely grated lemon zest
1 ripe banana, peeled and mashed
Seeds from 1/2 vanilla bean or 1/2 teaspoon vanilla extract
1 cup (128 g/4.5 oz) unbleached all-purpose flour
1/3 cup (58 g/2 oz) yellow cornmeal
1 1/2 teaspoons (7 g/0.25 oz) baking powder
1/4 teaspoon (1.6 g/0.06 oz) salt
1/2 cup (100 g/3.5 oz) turbinado sugar, for decorating

In the bowl of an electric mixer fitted with the paddle attachment, beat the vegan butter, sugar, rosemary, and lemon zest for 3 minutes, or until creamy. Beat in the banana and vanilla at medium speed until blended.

In a medium bowl, whisk together the flour, cornmeal, baking powder, and salt. Add the dry ingredients to the butter mixture, and mix at low speed just until combined. Form the dough into two 1-inch-wide logs. Wrap the logs in waxed paper and chill for 2 hours.

Preheat the oven to 325°F. Coat 2 baking sheets with nonstick cooking spray.

Slice the logs into 1/3-inch-thick rounds. Place turbinado sugar in a bowl and press one cut side of each cookie into the sugar. Arrange the cookies sugar side up on the baking sheets, spacing them 1 inch apart. Bake for 15 minutes, or until golden brown on the bottom. Transfer to wire racks to cool.

OATMEAL RAISIN CHILI COOKIES

Chewy and packed with oats and raisins, these oversized cookies are flavored with traditional spices, with just a hint of a bite from the addition of chili powder (which is thought to boost metabolism!). They have crispy edges and a soft center, which is how I like my oatmeal cookies, but if you prefer them crispier, bake them a few minutes longer, as directed below.

MAKES 18 LARGE COOKIES

1 cup (128 g/4.5 oz) unbleached all-purpose flour
1/2 teaspoon (2.5 g/0.09 oz) baking soda
1/2 teaspoon (1.5 g/0.05 oz) kosher salt
1 teaspoon (2 g/0.07 oz) ground cinnamon
1/2 teaspoon (1 g/0.03 oz) ground cloves
1/2 teaspoon (0.5 g/0.017 oz) freshly grated nutmeg
1/2 teaspoon (1 g/0.03 oz) chili powder
3/4 cup (170 g/6 oz) vegan butter
1 cup (216 g/7.6 oz) light brown sugar
1/2 cup (100 g/3.5 oz) Sucanat
1 teaspoon (5 g/0.17 oz) vanilla extract
1/2 cup (121 g/4.3 oz) soy milk
3 cups (240 g/8.5 oz) old-fashioned rolled oats (not quick-cooking)
1 cup (140 g/5 oz) black raisins

Position 2 racks near the center of the oven and preheat the oven to 350°F. Line 2 baking sheets with parchment paper or silicone baking mats.

In a medium bowl, whisk together the flour, baking soda, salt, and spices. Set aside.

In the bowl of an electric mixer fitted with the paddle attachment, beat the butter, brown sugar, Sucanat, and vanilla at high speed until smooth and light, about 2 minutes. Reduce the speed to low and mix in the soy milk until blended, scraping down the sides of the bowl as necessary (the mixture may separate and appear curdled at this point, which is okay). Add the dry ingredients gradually, mixing just until blended. Add the oats and raisins and mix just until blended.

Scoop 3 tablespoons of the batter (I use a 1¹/2-ounce ice cream scoop) and roll it into a 2-inch ball. Place the dough on one of the prepared baking sheets and flatten it slightly with your palm (wet your palm first to prevent it from sticking). Arrange a total of 6 discs of dough on each sheet, spacing them 3 inches apart, and bake for 18 to 22 minutes, switching the position of the sheets halfway through baking, until the cookies are nicely browned but still soft inside. (If you like them crunchy, bake for 2 to 4 minutes longer.) Cool the cookies on the baking sheet on a wire rack for 10 minutes, then transfer the cookies to the wire rack and cool completely.

THE SAVVY DIVA

Rolled oats are a great source of nutrients, including vitamin E, iron, zinc, selenium, magnesium, and copper. Adding rolled oats to baking recipes is a simple way to sneak in extra fiber while adding texture and chewiness to cookies and bars.

VEGAN CHOCOLATE CHIP COOKIES

These chewy-crunchy cookies are loaded with chocolate and are—trust me—quite addictive. The combination of turbinado and brown sugar gives them a toothsome crunch and a complex, caramel-like sweetness. I like to keep some dough in the freezer to bake whenever the urge strikes. To do this, shape it into a log, wrap it well in two layers of plastic, and freeze. Simply slice off 1/2-inch rounds from the log and bake as directed, adding on a couple of minutes to compensate for the coldness of the dough.

MAKES 60 COOKIES

2¼ cups (288 g/10.15 oz) unbleached all-purpose flour
1 teaspoon (5 g/0.17 oz) baking soda
½ teaspoon (1.5 g/0.05 oz) kosher salt
1 cup (202 g/7.1 oz) vegan butter spread
¾ cup (120 g/4.2 oz) turbinado sugar
¾ cup (162 g/5.7 oz) organic light brown sugar
1 tablespoon (12 g/0.42 oz) egg replacer mixed with
    ¼ cup (60 g/2.1 oz) warm water
1 teaspoon (4 g/0.14 oz) vanilla extract
1½ cups (255 g/9 oz) vegan semisweet chocolate morsels

Preheat the oven to 350°F.

In a medium bowl, sift together the flour and baking soda. Whisk in the salt and set aside.

In the bowl of an electric mixer fitted with the paddle attachment, cream the butter spread with the sugars at high speed until light, about 2 minutes. Add the egg replacer and water mixture and the vanilla and mix at medium speed until blended, stopping to scrape down the sides of the bowl with a rubber spatula as necessary. Reduce the speed to low and add the flour mixture gradually, mixing just until blended. Add the chocolate morsels and mix until evenly distributed.

Drop the dough by tablespoonfuls onto an ungreased baking sheet and bake for 9 to 12 minutes, until lightly browned around the edges. Cool on the sheet on a wire rack for 5 minutes, then transfer the cookies to the wire rack and cool completely.

CHOCOLATE HAZELNUT BISCOTTI

These deep chocolate biscotti are studded with toasted hazelnuts and rolled oats and accented with a hint of cinnamon. I love them because they are extra crunchy, making them the perfect accompaniment to a cup of espresso or coffee. This recipe can be doubled easily for a larger yield.

MAKES 36 BISCOTTI

BISCOTTI:
2 tablespoons (24 g/0.84 oz) pitted prunes, roughly chopped

¼ cup plus 2 tablespoons (30 g/1 oz) old-fashioned rolled oats
    (not quick-cooking)

⅓ cup (36 g/1.3 oz) chopped hazelnuts

⅔ cup (83 g/2.9 oz) whole wheat flour

⅓ cup (42 g/1.5 oz) unbleached all-purpose flour

½ cup (56 g/2 oz) unsweetened natural cocoa powder, sifted

¾ teaspoon (3.75 g/0.13 oz) baking powder

1 teaspoon (5 g/0.17 oz) baking soda

¼ teaspoon (0.75 g/0.025 oz) kosher salt

½ teaspoon (1 g/0.035 oz) ground cinnamon

¾ cup (6.15 oz/174 oz) lite silken tofu

½ cup (100 g/3.5 oz) evaporated cane juice sugar

½ tablespoon (6 g/0.21 oz) vanilla extract

¼ cup (60 g/2.1 oz) soy milk

CINNAMON TOPPING:
1 tablespoon (12 g/0.44 oz) light muscovado sugar

½ teaspoon (1 g/0.035 oz) ground cinnamon

Pinch of freshly grated nutmeg

MAKE THE BISCOTTI:

Position a rack near the center of the oven and preheat the oven to 350°F. Coat a baking sheet with nonstick cooking spray and set aside.

Combine the prunes and 1 tablespoon of water in a blender or food processor and process until smooth. Measure out 2 tablespoons prune puree and set aside (save the remainder for another use, such as adding to a smoothie).

Process the oats in a food processor until finely ground, about 30 seconds; set aside.

Scatter the hazelnuts in a single layer on another baking sheet. Toast for 5 to 7 minutes, until lightly browned, stirring once or twice. Remove from the oven and fold inside a clean kitchen towel. Set aside for 10 minutes, rubbing from time to time to remove the skins. Transfer the nuts to a small bowl.

In a large bowl, whisk together the ground oats, flours, and cocoa powder. Whisk in the baking powder, baking soda, salt, and cinnamon and set aside.

Put the tofu in the food processor and puree until smooth, about 30 seconds. Add the prune puree and sugar and process again until blended. Add the vanilla and soy milk and process until smooth. Fold the tofu mixture into the dry ingredients until blended, then fold in the hazelnuts.

Divide the dough in half and turn onto a lightly floured work surface. Shape each half into a 9-inch log that is 2 inches in diameter. Place the logs on the prepared baking sheet, spacing them 3 inches apart.

MAKE THE TOPPING AND BAKE THE BISCOTTI:
Combine all the topping ingredients in a small bowl. Sprinkle the topping over the logs, pressing it gently into the dough.

Bake the biscotti logs for 30 minutes, or until they are very firm to the touch and browned. Cool on the baking sheet on a wire rack for 10 minutes. Reduce the oven temperature to 325°F.

Using a metal spatula, transfer the logs to a work surface. Using a serrated knife, cut the logs diagonally into 1/2-inch-thick slices that are 3 to 4 inches long. Place the slices, cut side down, on the baking sheet (they can be tightly packed). Bake for 10 minutes. Turn the biscotti over and bake for 10 minutes more. Remove the biscotti from the oven, transfer to wire racks, and cool completely.

HOST LIKE A DIVA

In Italy, biscotti are typically served with a Tuscan fortified wine called Vin Santo, but here they are frequently served with espresso or coffee. Try stacking them on an elegant glass plate and serve at the end of a dinner party with coffee and digestifs.

PEANUT BUTTER CHOCOLATE CHIP SPELT COOKIES

These delicious peanut butter cookies are made with organic whole wheat spelt flour instead of standard wheat flour. Spelt is an ancient grain that is full of nutrients and is often tolerated by those who have sensitivities to regular wheat. In addition to the benefits of spelt, lots of crunchy, natural peanut butter and dark chocolate morsels make these cookies irresistible.

MAKES ABOUT 20 COOKIES

1 1/2 cups (360 g/12.7 oz) natural crunchy peanut butter
2 1/4 cups (281 g/9.9 oz) organic whole spelt flour
1 teaspoon (5 g/0.17 oz) baking soda
1 teaspoon (3 g/0.1 oz) kosher salt
1 1/2 cups (450 g/15.8 oz) maple syrup
2 teaspoons (10 g/0.35 oz) vanilla extract
1 1/2 cups (283 g/10 oz) vegan semisweet chocolate morsels

Position 2 racks near the center of the oven and preheat the oven to 375°F. Line 2 baking sheets with parchment paper or silicone baking mats.

Lightly coat a small saucepan with nonstick cooking spray and place the peanut butter in the pan over medium-low heat. Cook, stirring occasionally, until the peanut butter is fluid and smooth, about 5 minutes. Remove the pan from the heat.

In a medium bowl, gently whisk together the flour, baking soda, and salt and make a well in the center. Add the warm peanut butter, maple syrup, and vanilla to the well and stir until the dry ingredients are almost completely blended in. Add one third of the chocolate morsels, stir to combine, then add the remaining morsels gradually and mix until blended.

Scoop out about 2 tablespoons of the dough, forming it into rough 1 1/2-inch balls, and arrange them on the prepared baking sheets at least 2 inches apart. Using your palm (wet it first to prevent it from sticking), flatten each ball slightly. Bake the cookies for 15 to 17 minutes, switching the position of the sheets halfway through baking, until the cookies are golden brown. Cool on the sheets on wire racks for 10 minutes, then transfer the cookies to the racks and cool completely.

CHOCOLATE-COVERED MATZO WITH
SEA SALT AND ALMONDS

Matzo may be a little bit lacking in the flavor department, but its simplicity makes it ideal for all sorts of embellishments. Here I dress it up with a coating of vegan chocolate and top it with chopped toasted almonds, transforming something simple into something sensational. These are a great treat to bring to a Seder dinner during Passover. For a special presentation, wrap them in parchment paper, place them in a vintage can or Mason jar, and add a nice ribbon.

MAKES 7 MATZOS

7 unsalted matzo sheets
11 tablespoons (156 g/5.5 oz) vegan butter
3 tablespoons (40 g/1.4 oz) light brown sugar
1 cup (170 g/6 oz) vegan semisweet chocolate morsels
1/2 cup (53 g/1.8 oz) finely chopped toasted almonds
    (see page 199 for toasting instructions)
Fleur de sel for sprinkling on top

Preheat the oven to 350°F. Line 2 baking sheets with parchment paper. Arrange the matzos on the sheets, breaking them in half if necessary to fit them.

In a saucepan, combine the butter and brown sugar. Place over medium-high heat for 3 to 5 minutes, until the sugar is melted and the mixture is bubbly. Brush some of the mixture onto one side of each matzo. Bake the matzos, buttered side up, for 10 to 12 minutes, until they are golden brown. While the matzos are still hot, sprinkle the tops with the vegan chocolate morsels, dividing them evenly. Let them stand for 2 minutes, then spread the chocolate evenly over the matzos, covering them completely. Sprinkle the almonds and salt over the matzos and allow them to set for 15 minutes before serving. The matzos can be stored in an airtight container at room temperature for up to 5 days.

PINEAPPLE SQUARES

A touch of orange and coconut flavor accents the sunny pineapple topping in these tropical dessert bars. The topping is anchored by a tender baked crust, and a light dusting of confectioners' sugar makes a pretty finish. If you want more orange flavor, substitute orange juice for the pineapple juice.

MAKES 24 BARS

SHORTCRUST:
2 1/2 cups (320 g/11.3 oz) unbleached all-purpose flour

3/4 teaspoon (2.25 g/0.08 oz) kosher salt

2 tablespoons (25 g/0.88 oz) evaporated cane juice sugar

1/2 cup (113 g/4 oz) vegan butter, cut into 1/2-inch cubes and chilled

1/2 cup (96 g/3.4 oz) vegan shortening, chilled

1/4 cup plus 2 tablespoons (88 g/3.12 oz) ice-cold water

1 tablespoon (15 g/0.5 oz) apple cider vinegar

PINEAPPLE FILLING:
2 cups (483 g/17 oz) pineapple juice

1/2 cup (123 g/4.3 oz) canned crushed pineapple

3 tablespoons (22 g/0.8 oz) arrowroot powder

2 tablespoons (13 g/0.47 oz) agar agar powder

1/2 cup (100 g/3.5 oz) evaporated cane juice sugar

1/2 cup (150 g/5.3 oz) brown rice syrup

1/4 cup (60 g/2.1 oz) soy milk or coconut milk

2 teaspoons (8 g/0.28 oz) vanilla extract

1 1/2 teaspoons (6 g/0.21 oz) orange extract

1 tablespoon (14 g/0.5 oz) liquid coconut oil

Vegan confectioners' sugar for dusting

MAKE THE CRUST:
Preheat the oven to 350°F. Coat the bottom and sides of a 9-by-13-inch baking pan with nonstick cooking spray.

In a medium bowl, whisk together the flour, salt, and sugar. Add the butter cubes and shortening to the bowl and, using your fingers, mix them in until they are evenly distributed and the mixture is crumbly. Make a well in the center and add the water and vinegar to the well. Gradually stir the liquids into the dry ingredients with a wooden spoon or rubber spatula until you form a smooth dough. Place the dough in the prepared pan and, using your fingers, pat it into an even layer that covers the bottom of the pan. Using a fork, poke holes at 2-inch intervals all over the crust. Bake for 20 to 25 minutes, until golden around the edges. Place the pan on a wire rack to cool while you make the filling.

MAKE THE FILLING AND BAKE THE BARS:

Combine the pineapple juice, crushed pineapple, arrowroot, agar agar, sugar, brown rice syrup, soy milk, vanilla and orange extracts, and coconut oil in a medium saucepan over medium heat. Cook, whisking constantly, until the mixture starts to thicken, about 5 minutes. Pour the hot mixture over the baked crust. Refrigerate for 30 minutes, or until set. Sift vegan confectioners' sugar over the top, cut into squares, and serve.

THE SAVVY DIVA

Raw pineapple contains enzymes that prevent it from setting with gelling agents like agar agar. Cooking the fruit first, however, deactivates these enzymes, allowing the pineapple to gel. Since canned pineapple is heated during the canning process, it sets up perfectly.

SPICY GINGERSNAPS

These oversized gingersnaps are my favorite holiday cookies. Flavored with molasses, cinnamon, and a good amount of ginger, they feature a chewy texture and crackled, sugary top. They're ideal for an afternoon pick-me-up in December, or any other time of the year!

MAKES 18 LARGE COOKIES

    2 cups (256 g/9 oz) unbleached all-purpose flour
    1 tablespoon (9 g/0.32 oz) ground ginger
    2 teaspoons (10 g/0.35 oz) baking soda
    1 teaspoon (2 g/0.07 oz) ground cinnamon
    1/2 teaspoon (1.5 g/0.05 oz) kosher salt
    1/4 teaspoon (0.5 g/0.02 oz) ground black pepper
    3/4 cup (144 g/5 oz) vegan shortening
    2/3 cup plus 1/2 cup (233 g/4.7 oz) evaporated cane juice sugar
    1/3 cup firmly packed (71 g/2.5 oz) dark brown sugar
    3 tablespoons (45 g/1.6 oz) soy milk or rice milk
    1/4 cup (80 g/2.8 oz) unsulfured molasses

In a large bowl, whisk together the flour, ginger, baking soda, cinamon, salt, and pepper. Set aside.

In the bowl of an electric mixer fitted with the paddle attachment, cream the shortening with 2/3 cup of the cane juice sugar and the brown sugar at high speed until light, about 2 minutes. Reduce the speed to medium-low, add the soy or rice milk and molasses, and mix until completely blended and smooth, scraping down the sides of the bowl as necessary with a rubber spatula. At low speed, add the flour mixture 1/2 cup at a time, mixing after each addition, until a soft dough forms and no traces of flour remain. Scrape the dough out onto a work surface and shape it into a 9-inch-long log that is about 2 inches in diameter. Wrap the log tightly in plastic wrap and refrigerate for about 2 hours, until firm.

Position 2 racks near the center of the oven and preheat the oven to 350ºF. Line 2 baking sheets with parchment paper or silicone baking mats. Place the remaining 1/2 cup evaporated cane juice sugar in a shallow bowl.

Unwrap the dough log and slice it into $1/2$-inch-thick rounds, rolling the logs 90 degrees between cuts to keep the edges round. Dip one side of each slice in sugar, and arrange sugar side up on the prepared baking sheets, spacing the slices 2 inches apart. Bake the cookies for 11 to 13 minutes, switching the position of the sheets halfway through baking, until the cookies are crackled and dry on top. Cool for 10 minutes on the baking sheets on wire racks. Transfer the cookies to the racks and cool completely.

COCONUT MACAROONS

Coconut is one of my favorite flavors, and eating these moist little macaroons is one of my favorite ways to enjoy it. They taste just like non-vegan macaroons, but are made with better ingredients, including unsweetened coconut, evaporated cane juice sugar, and brown rice syrup. Another bonus is that these cookies might just be among the easiest in the world to make. Make sure you don't overbake them, though—their interiors should still be soft when you take them out of the oven.

MAKES 32 COOKIES

1 cup (200 g/7 oz) evaporated cane juice sugar

1/2 cup (121 g/4.2 oz) soy milk

2 tablespoons (40 g/1.4 oz) brown rice syrup

2 teaspoons (10 g/0.35 oz) vanilla extract

1 teaspoon (3 g/0.1 oz) kosher salt

3 cups (269 g/9.4 oz) unsweetened desiccated coconut (see Savvy Diva on page 52)

3/4 cup (96 g/3.3 oz) unbleached all-purpose flour

Position 2 racks near the center of the oven and preheat the oven to 350°F. Line 2 baking sheets with parchment paper or silicone baking mats.

In a medium bowl, stir together the sugar, soy milk, brown rice syrup, vanilla, and salt until well blended. Stir in the coconut. Add the flour and stir until well blended (the batter will be very thick at this point).

With your hands, form the batter into 1-inch balls and arrange them on the prepared baking sheet, spacing them 2 inches apart. Bake the macaroons for 14 to 16 minutes, switching the baking sheets halfway through baking, until they are golden brown and just set on the outside (they should still be soft inside). Repeat with any remaining batter. Cool the macaroons on the baking sheets on wire racks for 10 minutes, then transfer the cookies to the racks and cool completely.

Clockwise from left: Maple Pecan Sables (pages 48–49) and Coconut Macaroons, Toasted Coconut Cake (pages 92–94), Spicy Gingersnaps (pages 67–69), Chocolate Coffee Mini-Bundt Cakes (pages 106–108), Spicy Carrot Cake (pages 81–83), and Vegan Divas Chocolate Layer Cake (pages 88–90)

GIVRETTES AU CHOCOLAT

Givrettes, caramelized nuts that have been coated in chocolate and dusted with either cocoa powder or confectioners' sugar, are a classic French confection that I adore. I borrowed this recipe from my husband, François Payard, and though I admit it requires some attention to detail and patience, the results are well worth the effort. I like to pack givrettes in a cellophane bag and tie it with a pretty ribbon for a simple and elegant gift.

MAKES ABOUT 3¼ CUPS (400 G)

SPECIAL EQUIPMENT:
Instant-read thermometer

> ½ cup (100 g/3.5 oz) evaporated cane juice sugar
> 3 tablespoons (44 g/1.5 oz) water
> 2 cups (300 g/10.5 oz) whole unblanched almonds, hazelnuts,
>   or macadamia nuts, toasted (see page 199 for toasting instructions)
> 1 cup (170 g/6 oz) high-quality vegan bittersweet chocolate, finely chopped
> ⅓ cup (37 g/1.3 oz) unsweetened natural cocoa powder

Line a baking sheet with a silicone baking mat or piece of parchment paper. Combine the sugar and water in a medium, heavy-bottomed saucepan and bring to a boil over medium-high heat. Add the nuts and stir to coat them evenly with the syrup. Continue to cook, stirring constantly; the sugar will crystallize and turn sandy. Then, as you continue to stir, the sugar crystals will remelt and liquefy, gradually turning to a golden brown caramel. When most of the sandy sugar has melted, remove the pan from the heat.

Carefully spread the caramelized nuts onto the prepared baking sheet—they will be extremely hot. Let the nuts cool completely (if your baking sheet fits in the freezer, freeze the nuts until they have cooled). When cooled, break up any clusters of nuts with your hands. Place the nuts in a bowl and place the bowl in the freezer while you temper the chocolate.

To temper the chocolate, put about a third of it in a bowl and set aside. Have an instant-read thermometer at hand. Fill a medium pot one third full with water, place over medium heat, and bring to a gentle simmer. Place the chopped chocolate in a bowl that will fit snugly on top of the pot but not touch the water. Reduce the heat to low and place the bowl over the pot. Heat until the chocolate is completely melted, stirring occasionally with a silicone spatula. Once the chocolate has melted, stir in the reserved chocolate to lower the temperature. Set the chocolate aside in a cool place and let it stand, stirring occasionally. When its temperature reaches between 82° and 84°F, return the chocolate to the double boiler and briefly heat it until it reaches 87°F. The chocolate has now been tempered and is ready to use.

Remove the nuts from the freezer. While stirring them with a rubber spatula, add one third of the tempered chocolate to coat the nuts. Continue to stir the nuts with a spatula while slowly drizzling the remaining tempered chocolate over them. Continue to stir until the chocolate begins to set up and harden around the nuts.

Sift the cocoa powder over the nuts in the bowl and, using your hands (yes, this is a bit messy!), toss them until they are coated with cocoa powder (break up any clumps of nuts at the same time). Working with small batches, transfer the nuts to a fine-mesh sieve and shake them to remove any excess cocoa powder. Store the nuts in an airtight container at room temperature for up to a month.

THE SAVVY DIVA

When caramelizing sugar, always exercise great caution and have a bowl of cold water nearby, as the sugar gets extremely hot and can cause bad burns.

LEMON BARS

Made with fresh lemon juice and lemon and lime zest, these lemon bars are very tart, which is just the way I like them. This light and refreshing dessert is always welcome at a summer picnic or barbecue. A pretty dusting of confectioners' sugar and sprinkle of lime zest make these bars as elegant as they are delicious.

MAKES 18 WEDGES

CRUST:
1/2 cup (113 g/4 oz) vegan butter, at room temperature
1/4 cup (30 g/1 oz) vegan confectioners' sugar
1 cup (128 g/4.5 oz) unbleached all-purpose flour

LEMON FILLING:
1/2 cup (116 g/4 oz) silken tofu (soft or firm)
1 cup (200 g/7 oz) evaporated cane juice sugar
Finely grated zest of 2 lemons
Finely grated zest of 1 lime
1/3 cup (80 g/2.8 oz) fresh lemon juice (2 to 3 lemons)
2 tablespoons (16 g/0.56 oz) unbleached all-purpose flour
2 tablespoons (15 g/0.5 oz) cornstarch
Vegan confectioners' sugar, sifted, for garnish
Finely grated lime zest for garnish

Preheat the oven to 350°F. Coat an 8-inch square baking pan with nonstick cooking spray and sprinkle with a light dusting of flour.

MAKE THE CRUST:

In the bowl of an electric mixer fitted with the paddle attachment, cream the butter and confectioners' sugar at high speed for about 2 minutes, until light and fluffy. Reduce the speed to low, add the flour, and mix just until the dough comes together.

Press the crust mixture into the bottom of the prepared pan and bake for about 20 minutes, or until lightly browned. Remove the crust from the oven and place on a wire rack to cool while you make the filling.

MAKE THE FILLING:

Place the tofu in a blender or food processor and process until creamy, about 1 minute. Add the sugar and process until smooth. Add the lemon and lime zest, lemon juice, flour, and cornstarch and process until blended.

Pour the filling over the baked shortbread crust and bake for 30 minutes, or until the filling is set. Remove from the oven and place on a wire rack to cool (the filling will firm up as it cools).

To serve, cut into 9 squares, then cut each square in half diagonally to form triangles. Dust the triangles with the sifted confectioners' sugar and garnish with lime zest. Store in an airtight container at room temperature for up to 2 days.

part four

DIVA-LICIOUS
DESSERTS

LIME-RASPBERRY CHEESECAKE PIE

This tangy pie features a cheesecake filling flavored with fresh lime juice and a topping of fresh raspberries. The pie crust can be made in advance, and the filling, made from a base of tofu and vegan cream cheese, comes together in a flash in the food processor or blender. The result is an indulgent dessert that's worth every calorie.

MAKES ONE 9-INCH PIE, SERVING 8

Gingersnap Pie Crust (page 196) or
Basic Vegan Pie Crust (page 194)

CHEESECAKE FILLING:
One 12.3-oz (348-g) package extra-firm silken tofu
1 cup (210 g/7.4 oz) vegan cream cheese
½ cup (150 g/5.3 oz) maple syrup
1 teaspoon (4 g/0.14 oz) vanilla extract
1 tablespoon plus 1 teaspoon (8 g/0.28 oz)
    finely grated lime zest
Juice of 3 limes
2 teaspoons (2 g/0.07 oz) agar agar flakes
15 fresh raspberries for garnish

MAKE THE FILLING:
Preheat the oven to 350°F.

In a food processor, combine the tofu, cream cheese, maple syrup, vanilla, 1 tablespoon of the lime zest, and the lime juice; process until smooth, about 30 seconds. Add the agar agar flakes and process for about 1 minute, until completely blended and smooth.

Scrape the mixture into the prepared pie crust and place the pie on a baking sheet. Bake for 30 minutes, then turn off the oven and leave the pie in the oven for another 40 minutes.

Remove the pie from the oven, place on a wire rack, and cool completely.

Refrigerate the pie for at least 3 hours or overnight before serving. When ready to serve, garnish the top with raspberries, then sprinkle with the remaining 1 teaspoon lime zest.

HOST LIKE A DIVA

For restaurant-quality presentation of cakes, pies, tarts, and other desserts that are topped with fruit, warm up a little agave syrup in the microwave and brush it directly on the fruit before serving. The syrup makes the fruit glisten and your dessert will look like a masterpiece!

CHOCOLATE BUNDT CAKE

This simple Bundt cake is a great recipe to have in your baking repertoire: It's very chocolatey and satisfying, easy to make, and it travels well, so it's perfect for potlucks, school parties, or picnics. You can even dress it up for a dinner party by serving it with fresh berries and dairy-free ice cream.

MAKES ONE 10-INCH CAKE, SERVING 10 TO 12

3½ cups (448 g/15.8 oz) unbleached all-purpose flour
¾ cup plus 3 tablespoons (105 g/3.7 oz) unsweetened natural
    cocoa powder, sifted
1⅓ cups (266 g/9.4 oz) evaporated cane juice sugar
1½ teaspoons (7.5 g/0.26 oz) baking soda
1 teaspoon (3 g/0.1 oz) kosher salt
2 cups (472 g/16.6 oz) water
½ cup (108 g/3.8 oz) liquid coconut oil
1½ teaspoons (6 g/0.21 oz) vanilla extract
1½ teaspoons (6 g/0.21 oz) apple cider vinegar
Vegan confectioners' sugar for dusting (optional)

Preheat the oven to 375°F. Coat a 10-cup Bundt pan with nonstick cooking spray.

In a large bowl, whisk together the flour, cocoa powder, cane juice sugar, baking soda, and salt. Set aside.

In a medium bowl, stir together the water, oil, vanilla, and vinegar. Pour the wet ingredients into the dry ones and stir just until blended (do not overmix; the batter will be thick). Scrape the batter into the prepared pan and bake for 35 minutes, or until a toothpick inserted into the center of the cake comes out clean. Cool the cake in the pan on a wire rack for 20 minutes, then invert onto the rack and cool completely.

Sift the confectioners' sugar over the top just before serving.

SPICY CARROT CAKE

My vegan version of this much-loved cake is made with a combination of whole wheat and white flour, and is well spiced with cardamom, cinnamon, nutmeg, and ginger. Crushed pineapple, coconut oil, and lots of shredded carrots ensure that the cake is extra-moist, while a fluffy cream cheese frosting is, well, the frosting on the cake!

MAKES ONE 8-INCH LAYER CAKE, SERVING 8

1 1/2 cups (188 g/6.6 oz) whole wheat flour

1/2 cup (64 g/2.2 oz) unbleached all-purpose flour

2 teaspoons (10 g/0.34 oz) baking powder

1 teaspoon (5 g/0.17 oz) baking soda

1 1/4 cups (250 g/8.8 oz) evaporated cane juice sugar

1 cup (246 g/8.6 oz) canned crushed pineapple (with juice)

2/3 cup (160 g/5.6 oz) soy yogurt

1/4 cup (56 g/2 oz) liquid coconut oil

2 teaspoons (10 g/0.34 oz) vanilla extract

1 teaspoon (3 g/0.1 oz) ground cardamom

1 teaspoon (5 g/0.18 oz) ground cinnamon

1 teaspoon (5 g/0.18 oz) freshly grated nutmeg

1 teaspoon (5 g/0.18 oz) ground ginger

1 teaspoon (3 g/0.1 oz) kosher salt

2 cups (180 g/6.34 oz) shredded organic carrots (about 2 medium carrots)

1/2 cup (70 g/2.4 oz) golden raisins

1/2 cup (56 g/2 oz) chopped walnuts

Vegan Cream Cheese Frosting (page 198)

MAKE THE CAKE:

Preheat the oven to 350°F. Coat the bottom and sides of two 8-inch cake pans with nonstick cooking spray and set aside.

In a large bowl, whisk together the whole wheat flour, all-purpose flour, baking powder, and baking soda; set aside.

In a medium bowl, stir together the sugar, crushed pineapple, soy yogurt, coconut oil, vanilla, cardamom, cinnamon, nutmeg, ginger, and salt until well blended.

Stir the pineapple mixture into the dry ingredients until blended. Stir in the shredded carrots, raisins, and walnuts.

Scrape the batter into the prepared cake pans and bake for 25 to 30 minutes, until a toothpick inserted into the centers of the cakes comes out clean. Cool the cakes in the pans on a wire rack for 15 minutes. Invert the cakes onto the rack and cool completely.

FROST THE CAKE:

Place one of the cake layers on a cardboard round or a flat plate and cover with a gener-ous layer of frosting, spreading it to the edges of the cake with a metal spatula. Top with the remaining layer, then frost the top and sides of the cake with the remaining frosting.

The Savvy Diva

Carrot juice is packed with vitamins, so I try to drink some every day. I love to mix it with fresh ginger for a zingy drink. Never store carrot juice for more than a day, as it attracts bacteria and spoils quickly.

MANGO PINEAPPLE CAKE

Mangoes are considered the queen of tropical fruit in Brazil, and mango trees grow throughout my homeland. I love the sweet, musky flavor of the fruit, and frequently feature it in my desserts, as I do in this festive cake. The cake layers are made with mango puree, which gives them a yellow color that is contrasted with bright chunks of Maraschino cherries. A lush coconut cream and crushed pineapple complete the tropical flavor profile of this delicious layer cake.

MAKES ONE 8-INCH LAYER CAKE, SERVING 10 TO 12

MANGO CAKE:

2 cups (256 g/9 oz) all-purpose flour

2 teaspoons (5 g/0.17 oz) cornstarch

2½ teaspoons (12.5 g/0.44 oz) baking powder

1 large (538 g/19 oz) ripe mango

12 tablespoons (170 g/6 oz) vegan butter

1 cup (200 g/7 oz) evaporated cane juice sugar

1½ cups (363 g/12.8 oz) soy milk

¼ cup (44 g/1.5 oz) canned or fresh dark Maraschino cherries, pitted and chopped

¼ cup (28 g/1 oz) chopped walnuts

ASSEMBLY:

Coconut Whipped Cream (page 197) or 1½ cups non-dairy whipped topping

2 cups canned crushed pineapple, drained

MAKE THE CAKE:

Preheat the oven to 350°F. Coat two 8-inch cake pans with nonstick cooking spray.

In a medium bowl, sift together the flour, cornstarch, and baking powder and whisk to combine.

Using a sharp knife, slice the sides off the mango on either side of the pit. Cut the flesh in each pitless mango piece lengthwise and crosswise just down to the skin (don't cut through the skin) to form small squares of flesh. Then, holding the knife horizontal to the skin, slice the mango squares off the skin. Place them in a food processor or blender

and process until smooth. You will need ¾ cup mango puree for the cake. Set the puree aside.

In the bowl of an electric mixer fitted with the paddle attachment, beat the vegan butter with the cane juice sugar at medium speed until well blended, about 2 minutes. Add the reserved mango puree and mix until blended, scraping down the sides of the bowl with a rubber spatula as necessary to ensure the mixture is evenly blended (the mixture will look curdled at this point). Reduce the speed to low and add the dry ingredients in 3 additions, alternating with the soy milk in 2 additions and mixing just until blended. Remove the bowl from the mixer stand and fold in the Maraschino cherries and walnuts by hand. Divide the batter between the prepared pans and bake for 35 to 40 minutes, until the cakes are golden and a toothpick inserted into the center of each comes out clean. Cool the cakes in the pans on wire racks for 15 minutes, then invert them onto the racks and cool completely.

ASSEMBLE THE CAKE:

Place one of the cake layers on a cake plate and frost the top with half of the Coconut Whipped Cream, leaving an inch border around the edge. Spoon half of the crushed pineapple on top of the cream and top with the remaining cake layer. Frost the top with the remaining cream and garnish the top with the remaining crushed pineapple.

THE SAVVY DIVA

Choose mangoes that yield slightly when pressed and that have a smooth skin and full aroma. Mangoes can range in color from green to red, but those that have some yellow color in their skin are the most flavorful.

CHOCOLATE PUDDING CAKE

One of the greatest things about this decadent chocolate dessert is that you don't even have to turn on the oven to make it! The pudding only takes about 30 minutes to whip together, and then just needs a few hours in the refrigerator to set up before serving. Somewhere between a cake and a pudding, it has soft mousse-like texture that melts in your mouth. I like to serve it with Coconut Whipped Cream (page 197) or a store-bought dairy-free whipped topping.

MAKES ONE 8-INCH LAYER "CAKE," SERVING 12 TO 14

17.6 ounces (500 g) vegan bittersweet chocolate, such as Callebaut, finely chopped
2 cups (484 g/17 oz) soy milk
1/2 teaspoon (2 g/0.07 oz) vanilla extract
1 1/2 cups (350 g/12.3 oz) soft silken tofu, drained
Coconut Whipped Cream (page 197) or
    vegan whipped topping for serving

Coat an 8-inch springform pan with nonstick cooking spray and line the bottom of the pan with a round of parchment paper.

Place the chopped chocolate in a large bowl and set aside.

Place the soy milk in a small saucepan and bring to a boil over medium-high heat. Pour the hot milk over the chocolate and allow to stand for 1 minute. Whisk until the chocolate is completely melted and smooth. Stir in the vanilla.

Place the tofu in a blender or food processor and process until creamy. Fold the tofu into the chocolate mixture until well blended. Scrape the mixture into the prepared pan and smooth it into an even layer with a rubber spatula. Refrigerate the cake for at least 4 hours, until firm.

Hold a small paring knife under hot water for several seconds and then wipe it dry. Run the warm knife around the edge of the pan to release the cake, and remove the side of the pan. Cut into slices and serve with Coconut Whipped Cream or other vegan whipped topping.

VEGAN DIVAS CHOCOLATE LAYER CAKE

Vegans and non-vegans alike will love this over-the-top chocolate cake. It's a classic American layer cake—super-moist chocolate layers frosted with our popular Vegan Divas Chocolate Mousse, which has been thickened with a little cocoa powder. Make this for a birthday or any special occasion for the chocolate lover in your life.

Makes one 9-inch cake, serving 12

CHOCOLATE CAKE LAYERS:
2 cups (256 g/9 oz) unbleached all-purpose flour
1½ cups (170 g/6 oz) unsweetened natural cocoa powder
2¼ tablespoons (27 g/0.9 oz) baking powder
2¼ tablespoons (27 g/0.9 oz) baking soda
¾ teaspoon (2.25 g/0.08 oz) kosher salt
1 cup plus 2 tablespoons (258 g/9.2 oz) extra-firm tofu
1 cup plus 2 tablespoons (266 g/9.3 oz) water
½ cup plus 2 tablespoons (134 g/4.7 oz) liquid coconut oil
1 cup (242 g/8.5 oz) soy milk
1 cup (296 g/10.4 oz) maple syrup
1½ tablespoons (18 g/0.6 oz) vanilla extract
1½ tablespoons (22 g/0.8 oz) apple cider vinegar

FROSTING:
Vegan Divas Chocolate Mousse (page 117)
2 tablespoons (14 g/0.5 oz) unsweetened natural cocoa powder

MAKE THE CAKE LAYERS:
Preheat the oven to 325°F. Coat the bottom and sides of two 9-inch round cake pans with nonstick cooking spray and set aside.

In a large bowl, whisk together the flour, cocoa powder, baking powder, baking soda, and salt. Set aside.

In the bowl of a food processor, process the tofu and water until smooth, about 40 seconds. Place the mixture in another medium bowl and whisk in the coconut oil, soy milk, maple syrup, vanilla, and vinegar. Whisk in the dry ingredients until blended. Divide the batter between the pans and bake for 20 to 25 minutes, until a toothpick inserted into the centers of the cakes comes out clean. Cool the cakes in the pans on wire racks for 15 minutes, then invert the cakes onto the racks and cool completely.

MAKE THE FROSTING:

Prepare the Vegan Divas Chocolate Mousse as directed, but do not refrigerate it yet. Add the cocoa powder to the mousse and process in the food processor until blended. Refrigerate the frosting just until the cake layers are completely cooled.

FROST THE CAKE:

Place one of the cake layers on a cardboard cake round or serving plate and top with a layer of frosting. Top with the other cake layer and frost the top and sides of the cake with the remaining frosting. Serve immediately or refrigerate until ready to serve.

HOST LIKE A DIVA

To cut the perfect cake slice, fill a container with warm water and dip a sharp, nonserrated knife into it, wiping the blade dry with a paper towel before cutting. Continue to clean your knife with a wet paper towel after cutting each slice. I like to serve cake slices on simple white china for an elegant presentation.

TOASTED COCONUT CAKE

I love the deep, nutty flavor of toasted coconut, especially in this moist layer cake, which gets an added depth of flavor from maple syrup. A rich cream cheese frosting and a garnish of additional toasted coconut elevates this cake to the realm of something spectacular.

MAKES ONE 9-INCH CAKE, SERVING 12

COCONUT CAKE LAYERS:
2½ cups (320 g/11.28 oz) unbleached all-purpose flour

½ cup (45 g/1.6 oz) unsweetened desiccated coconut,
   toasted (see page 199 for toasting instructions)

2¼ teaspoons (11 g/0.4 oz) baking powder

1 teaspoon (5 g/0.17 oz) baking soda

¾ teaspoon (2.25 g/0.08 oz) kosher salt

¾ cup (177 g/6.2 oz) tofu water (see page 188)

¾ cup plus 2 tablespoons (140 g/5 oz) liquid coconut oil

¾ cup plus 2 tablespoons (210 g/7.4 oz) soy milk

1¼ cups (375 g/13.2 oz) maple syrup

1 tablespoon (15 g/0.5 oz) vanilla extract

1 tablespoon (15 g/0.5 oz) coconut extract

1⅛ teaspoons (5.6 g/0.2 oz) apple cider vinegar

Vegan Cream Cheese Frosting (page 198)

GARNISH:
½ cup (45 g/1.6 oz) unsweetened desiccated coconut, toasted
   (see page 199 for toasting instructions)

MAKE THE CAKE LAYERS:

Preheat the oven to 325°F. Coat two 9-inch round cake pans with nonstick cooking spray and set aside.

In a large bowl, gently whisk together the flour, toasted coconut, baking powder, baking soda, and salt until combined. Form a well in the center of the dry ingredients. Add the

tofu water, coconut oil, soy milk, maple syrup, vanilla and coconut extracts, and vinegar to the center. Gradually whisk together the liquid and dry ingredients until blended. Evenly divide the batter between the prepared cake pans and bake for 18 to 22 minutes, until the tops of the cakes are golden and a toothpick inserted into the centers of the cakes comes out clean. Cool the layers in the pans on wire racks for 15 minutes, then invert them onto the racks and cool completely.

FROST AND GARNISH THE CAKE:

Place one of the cake layers on a cardboard cake round or serving plate. Frost the top of the cake with a layer of the frosting, bringing it right to the edge of the cake. Top with the other cake layer and frost the top and sides of the cake with the remaining frosting. Pat the toasted coconut around the sides of the cake. Serve the cake at room temperature. Store, loosely covered, in the refrigerator for up to a week.

SOY PUDDING WITH BLUEBERRY SAUCE

There are lots of versions of soy pudding around, but this one is my favorite because it's so simple and it can be unmolded onto a plate for an elegant presentation. I serve it with a glistening blueberry sauce that can be made up to 5 days in advance—just warm it up right before serving.

SERVES 8

SOY PUDDING:

4 teaspoons (9 g/0.3 oz) agar agar powder

3⅓ cups (806 g/28.4 oz) soy milk

¼ cup (75 g/2.6 oz) maple syrup

BLUEBERRY SAUCE:

⅓ cup (50 g/1.75 oz) dried blueberries

1 cup (236 g/8.3 oz) water

2 tablespoons (30 g/1 oz) fresh lemon juice

2 tablespoons (37 g/1.3 oz) maple syrup

MAKE THE PUDDING:

In a small saucepan, whisk the agar agar powder into the soy milk until the agar agar is completely dissolved. Whisk in the maple syrup, place the pan over medium-high heat, and bring to a boil. Remove from the heat, divide the mixture among eight 4-ounce ramekins, and refrigerate until set, about 30 minutes.

MAKE THE SAUCE:

In a small saucepan, combine the dried blueberries, water, lemon juice, and maple syrup and bring to a boil over medium-high heat. Reduce the heat to low so that the mixture is barely simmering and simmer for 20 to 30 minutes, until it is the consistency of a thick sauce. Cool slightly before serving.

TO SERVE:

The puddings can either be served in the ramekins, with a little sauce on top, or they can be unmolded. To unmold, run a paring knife around the edge of each pudding and invert onto a plate. Spoon some sauce on top of the pudding or on the plate.

RAW CHOCOLATE AVOCADO TART

Avocado and chocolate might seem like an odd flavor pairing, but they work wonderfully together in this rich, no-bake tart. Anchored by a crunchy chocolate pecan crust, the chocolate filling is half mousse, half pudding, with a silky texture courtesy of the avocado. This tart is a snap to make and comes together in the food processor in minutes.

MAKES ONE 9-INCH TART, SERVING 10 TO 12

CHOCOLATE CRUST:

2 cups (200 g/7 oz) pecan halves

1/4 cup (28 g/1 oz) unsweetened natural cocoa powder

2 tablespoons (28 g/1 oz) liquid coconut oil

1/4 cup (74 g/2.6 oz) maple syrup

1 teaspoon (4 g/0.14 oz) vanilla extract

1/2 teaspoon (1.5 g/0.05 oz) kosher salt

CHOCOLATE AVOCADO MOUSSE:

1 cup plus 2 tablespoons (191 g/6.7 oz) vegan
    semisweet chocolate morsels

3 small, ripe avocados, pitted and flesh scooped out

1 tablespoon (7 g/0.25 oz) arrowroot powder

1/4 teaspoon (0.75 g/0.026 oz) kosher salt

1 teaspoon (4 g/0.14 oz) vanilla extract

1/4 cup (28 g/1 oz) unsweetened natural cocoa powder,
    sifted

1/3 cup (80 g/2.8 oz) almond milk

2/3 cup (198 g/7 oz) maple syrup

1 tablespoon (15 g/0.5 oz) smooth peanut butter

MAKE THE CRUST:

Brush the bottom and sides of a 9 1/2-inch springform pan with vegetable oil and line the bottom with a circle of parchment paper.

In a food processor, pulse the pecans until crumbly (you should have some finely ground pecans and some pieces no larger than 1/4 inch). Add the remaining crust ingredients and pulse until just mixed. Scoop the mixture into the prepared pan and press it onto the bottom with slightly wet fingers or a spatula. Place the crust in the freezer to set while you make the mousse.

MAKE THE MOUSSE:

Place the chocolate in a medium microwave-safe bowl and microwave on medium (50%) power for about 3 minutes, stopping to stir it every 45 seconds. Set the melted chocolate aside to cool slightly.

Combine all the remaining mousse ingredients except the melted chocolate in a food processor and process until smooth. Add the melted chocolate and process until smooth.

Remove the crust from the freezer and pour the mousse into it. Smooth it into an even layer and freeze, uncovered, for about 2 hours until firm.

SERVE THE TART:

Remove the tart from the freezer and unclasp and remove the side of the pan. Place the tart on a serving plate and allow it to stand at room temperature for 10 minutes before serving.

APPLESAUCE CAKE

This could be the easiest cake you'll ever make, but its simplicity belies its deliciousness. Lots of pure, organic applesauce makes it really moist, and gives it a straight-from-the-apple-orchard flavor. Made with fiber-rich whole wheat flour, it only has a little added sweetener and uses very little oil—so you won't feel guilty about eating a second piece (and believe me, you will!). I love to eat this cake warm, straight from the oven. It's the perfect partner to afternoon coffee or tea.

MAKES ONE 8-INCH CAKE, SERVING ABOUT 9

2 cups (250 g/8.8 oz) whole wheat flour
1/2 teaspoon (1.5 g/0.05 oz) kosher salt
1 1/2 teaspoons (7.5 g/0.26 oz) baking soda
1 teaspoon (2 g/0.07 oz) ground cinnamon
1/3 cup (71 g/2.5 oz) liquid coconut oil
3/4 cup (150 g/5.3 oz) evaporated cane juice sugar
1 1/2 cups (363 g/12.8 oz) organic unsweetened applesauce

Preheat the oven to 350°F. Coat an 8-inch square baking pan with nonstick cooking spray.

In a medium bowl, whisk together the flour, salt, baking soda, and cinnamon.

In another medium bowl, whisk together the oil and sugar. Whisk in the applesauce. Gently whisk in the dry ingredients until blended. Scrape the batter into the prepared pan and bake for 35 to 40 minutes, until the cake is nicely browned and a toothpick inserted into the center comes out clean. Cool the cake in the pan on a wire rack or serve warm. Cut the cake into squares straight from the pan to serve.

THE SAVVY DIVA

Applesauce freezes very well and can be stored in an airtight container in the freezer for up to 6 months. Thaw it in the refrigerator overnight or, if you're in a hurry, microwave it on 50% power for a few minutes, stirring occasionally.

PUMPKIN PIE

After living in the US for several years, I've come to understand that Thanksgiving without pumpkin pie is, well, downright un-American. But this silky pie is so good, you'll probably want to eat it more often than once a year. Make sure to use a deep-dish pie pan so there will be enough room for all the gorgeous pumpkin filling.

MAKES ONE 9-INCH PIE, SERVING 8

Basic Vegan Pie Crust (page 194), prepared in a deep-dish pie pan

PUMPKIN FILLING:
2¼ cups (510 g/18 oz) drained soft silken tofu
1 cup (240 g/8.4 oz) canned organic pumpkin puree
1 cup plus 1 tablespoon (227 g/8 oz) cold vegan cream cheese, cut into 1-inch chunks
1¼ cups (250 g/8.8 oz) evaporated cane juice sugar
½ teaspoon (0.5 g/0.02 oz) freshly grated nutmeg
½ teaspoon (1 g/0.03 oz) ground cinnamon
½ teaspoon (1 g/0.03 oz) ground cloves
1 tablespoon (15 g/0.5 oz) vanilla extract

Preheat the oven to 325°F.

Place the tofu and pumpkin puree in the bowl of a food processor and process until smooth, about 45 seconds. Add the chunks of cream cheese and the remaining ingredients and process until smooth and creamy, about 1 minute. Pour the mixture into the prepared pie crust and bake the pie for 50 to 55 minutes, until just set in the center (it will still be slightly jiggly but should not be liquid). Turn the oven off and leave the pie in the oven for another 30 minutes. Transfer to a wire rack and cool completely.

Refrigerate the pie for at least 4 hours or overnight before serving.

HOST LIKE A DIVA

For a truly authentic Thanksgiving experience, you can serve a bowl of my fluffy Coconut Whipped Cream (page 197) alongside this pie or, in a pinch, simply buy some vegan whipped topping to scoop or pipe on top.

SUGAR-FREE CARROT CAKE

Okay, I know there's already a carrot cake recipe in this book, but I couldn't stop at just one, and here's why: It's hard to find a recipe for a sugar-free cake that isn't full of artificial sweeteners! I love this cake, which is sweetened with Medjool dates, golden raisins, and orange juice concentrate. Made with whole wheat flour, fresh carrots, and zero added fat, it makes a great go-to cake for any occasion.

MAKES ONE 9-INCH CAKE, SERVING 10 TO 12

2 cups (250 g/8.8 oz) whole wheat flour
1 teaspoon (5 g/0.17 oz) baking powder
1 teaspoon (5 g/0.17 oz) baking soda
1/4 teaspoon (0.75 g/0.026 oz) kosher salt
1 1/4 cups (295 g/10.4 oz) water
1 cup (167 g/5.9 oz) chopped pitted Medjool dates
1 cup (149 g/5.2 oz) golden raisins
1 teaspoon (2 g/0.07 oz) ground cinnamon
1 teaspoon (2 g/0.07 oz) ground ginger
1/2 teaspoon (1 g/0.035 oz) ground cloves
1/2 teaspoon (1 g/0.035 oz) ground nutmeg
1/2 cup (90 g/3.17 oz) grated carrots (about 1 medium carrot)
1/3 cup (77 g/2.7 oz) frozen orange juice concentrate, thawed
Vegan confectioners' sugar for dusting (optional)

Coat a 9-inch round cake pan with nonstick cooking spray.

In a medium bowl, whisk together the flour, baking powder, baking soda, and salt and set aside.

In a small saucepan, combine the water, dates, raisins, cinnamon, ginger, cloves, and nutmeg. Bring to a boil over high heat, then reduce the heat to low and gently simmer for 5 minutes.

Place the shredded carrots in a large bowl, pour the date mixture over them, and allow to cool completely. While the mixture is cooling, preheat the oven to 375°F.

Add the orange juice concentrate to the cooled carrot mixture and mix well. Add the dry ingredients to the wet ingredients and stir well to combine. Scrape the batter into the prepared pan and bake for 30 to 35 minutes, until a toothpick inserted in the center comes out clean. Cool the cake in the pan on a wire rack for 10 minutes, then invert the cake onto the rack and cool completely.

Dust with sifted confectioners' sugar over the top before serving, if desired.

THE SAVVY DIVA

Before chopping the dates, lightly coat the blade of your knife with nonstick cooking spray. This will prevent the dates from sticking to it as you chop.

part five

LET'S HAVE A
PARTY

CHOCOLATE-COFFEE MINI BUNDT CAKES

The texture of these cute little Bundt cakes is more like custard than cake, and their deep chocolate flavor will satisfy the most demanding chocophile. The coffee is more of a back note here—it rounds out the flavor of the chocolate by cutting its sweetness. If you want a more pronounced coffee flavor, use strongly brewed coffee. These cakes really need no adornment, but a light dusting of confectioners' sugar gives them a finished look.

MAKES 12 MINI-BUNDT CAKES

1½ cups (192 g/6.7 oz) unbleached all-purpose flour
1 cup (200 g/7 oz) evaporated cane juice sugar
¾ cup (84 g/3 oz) unsweetened natural cocoa powder, sifted
1 teaspoon (5 g/0.17 oz) baking powder
¾ teaspoon (3.75 oz/1.8 oz) baking soda
½ teaspoon (1.5 g/0.05 oz) kosher salt
2 tablespoons (24 g/0.84 oz) liquid coconut oil
2 tablespoons (24 g/0.84 oz) vegan shortening
¼ cup (48 g/1.7 oz) egg replacer mixed with 1 cup water
1½ teaspoons (6 g/0.21 oz) vanilla extract
1 cup (242 g/8.5 oz) almond milk or soy milk
1 cup (236 g/8.3 oz) brewed coffee, at room temperature
¼ cup (43 g/1.5 oz) vegan semisweet chocolate morsels
Vegan confectioners' sugar, for dusting (optional)

Preheat the oven to 375°F. Coat two 6-cup mini-Bundt pans with nonstick cooking spray.

In a large bowl, whisk together the flour, cane juice sugar, cocoa powder, baking powder, baking soda, and salt. Set aside.

In the bowl of an electric mixer fitted with the whisk attachment, beat the coconut oil, shortening, egg substitute mixture, and vanilla at high speed until emulsified, about 2 minutes. Whisk together the almond or soy milk and the coffee in a large bowl and gradually whisk in half of the dry mixture. Whisk in the coconut oil mixture, then whisk in the remaining dry ingredients. Stir in the chocolate morsels. Divide the batter into the prepared mini Bundt cups and bake for 30 to 40 minutes, until a toothpick inserted into the centers of the cakes comes out clean (be aware that you may hit a melted chocolate morsel!). Cool the cakes in the pans on wire racks for 20 minutes, then invert the cakes onto the racks and cool completely. Dust with sifted confectioners' sugar if desired.

HOST LIKE A DIVA

When dusting desserts with confectioners' sugar, I like to wait until just before the dessert is served—if you dust too early, the sugar can be absorbed by the oil in the cake, which not only causes you to lose the pretty snow-white effect, but can also make the cake soggy. When serving a cake in wedges or slices, it can be nice to sift a little confectioners' sugar on individual plated slices.

COCONUT LIME ICE CREAM

This ice cream is the perfect refreshing end to a summer dinner party. Because it lacks dairy and fat, the ice cream tends to be quite hard when taken directly from the freezer. I recommend defrosting it slightly in the refrigerator for about 15 to 20 minutes before serving to make scooping easier.

MAKES ABOUT 1¾ PINTS (850 G)

SPECIAL EQUIPMENT:
Ice cream maker

One 12-oz (340-g) container soft silken tofu
¾ cup (181 g/6.4 oz) soy milk
½ cup plus 1 tablespoon (121 g/4.2 oz) vegetable oil
¾ cup (150 g/5.3 oz) evaporated cane juice sugar
2 tablespoons (37 g/1.3 oz) organic shredded coconut
2¼ teaspoons (12 g/0.4 oz) vanilla extract
¼ cup (25 g/0.88 oz) finely grated lime zest

In the bowl of a food processor, combine all the ingredients except the lime zest and process until creamy, about 1 minute. Transfer the mixture to a medium bowl and stir in the lime zest.

Process the mixture in an ice cream machine according to the manufacturer's instructions. Store in the freezer in an airtight container for up to 2 weeks.

GLUTEN-FREE RASPBERRY CHEESECAKE IN A GLASS

This cheesecake parfait is composed of layers of vegan sour cream, fresh raspberries, and tender gluten-free raspberry-and-lemon-flavored cookies. Since it's served in a glass and can be made up to 6 hours in advance, it makes a great dinner party dessert that can be taken straight from fridge to table.

SERVES 6

GLUTEN-FREE RASPBERRY LEMON
CHEESECAKE COOKIES:
1 tablespoon (10 g/0.35 oz) golden flax seeds
2 tablespoons (30 g/1 oz) warm water
1/3 cup (64 g/2.2 oz) liquid coconut oil
1/3 cup (80 g/2.8 oz) vegan cream cheese, softened
1/2 cup evaporated cane juice sugar or turbinado sugar
11/2 cups (213 g/7.5 oz) fresh raspberries
Zest of 1/2 small lemon
1 cup (128 g/4.5 oz) gluten-free all-purpose flour
1 teaspoon (5 g/0.17 oz) baking powder
1/2 teaspoon (1.25 g/0.04 oz) xanthan gum or agar agar flakes
Pinch of salt

ASSEMBLY:
21/4 cups (544 g/19.2 oz) vegan sour cream
2 cups (280 g/10 oz) fresh raspberries

MAKE THE COOKIES:

Preheat the oven to 350°F. Line a baking sheet with parchment paper or a silicone baking mat.

Grind the flax seeds in a coffee grinder or blender until finely ground. Place the ground flax in a small bowl, add the warm water, and stir. Place in the refrigerator to set until ready to use. (This equals/replaces one egg.)

In the bowl of an electric mixer fitted with the paddle attachment, cream together the coconut oil, cream cheese, and cane juice or turbinado sugar at medium-high speed for

2 minutes, or until smooth. Remove the bowl from the mixer stand and stir in the flax mixture, the raspberries, and the lemon zest.

In a small bowl, combine the flour, baking powder, xanthan gum or agar agar, and salt and stir the dry ingredients into the cream cheese mixture to form a firm dough. Roll the dough into 1¼-inch balls and arrange them on the prepared baking sheet 1 inch apart. Using your palm, flatten the balls so that they are ⅓ inch thick. Bake for 13 to 15 minutes, until they are just beginning to turn golden around the edges (the cookies should be soft inside). Transfer the cookies to a wire rack and cool completely.

ASSEMBLE THE DESSERTS:

Spoon 2 tablespoons of the sour cream into the bottom of a dessert glass. Top with 5 or 6 raspberries, another layer of sour cream, a cookie (if the cookie is too large to fit, trim it with a cookie cutter), and another layer of sour cream. Garnish the top of the dessert with a few more raspberries. Repeat to make a total of 6 desserts. Refrigerate until ready to serve.

ESPRESSO-LEMON PANNA COTTA

I love the pairing of espresso and lemon in this sleek layered panna cotta—the lemon flavor softens the bitterness of the espresso and adds a fresh flavor. Make sure that the agar agar flakes are completely dissolved before pouring the mixture into the glasses. If they aren't, they will sink to the bottom and the dessert won't set up properly.

SERVES 4

LEMON LAYER:

1 cup (232 g/8.18 oz) soy creamer

1 cup (242 g/8.5 oz) soy milk

¼ cup plus 2 tablespoons (81 g/2.8 oz) packed light brown sugar

2 teaspoons (8 g/0.3 oz) vanilla extract

½ teaspoon (1 g/0.03 oz) lemon zest

Pinch of freshly grated nutmeg

2 teaspoons (4.5 g/0.16 oz) agar agar flakes

ESPRESSO LAYER:

⅔ cup (154 g/5.4 oz) soy creamer

½ cup (121 g/4.2 oz) soy milk

¼ cup (50 g/1.76 oz) evaporated cane juice sugar

1 teaspoon (4 g/0.14 oz) vanilla extract

1 teaspoon (2.25 g/0.08 oz) agar agar flakes

2 to 4 tablespoons (30–60 g/1–2 oz) espresso,
   depending on how strong you want it

GARNISH:

Non-dairy whipped topping or Coconut Whipped Cream (page 197)

Finely grated lemon zest

MAKE THE LEMON LAYER:

Mix together the soy creamer, soy milk, brown sugar, vanilla, lemon zest, and nutmeg in a saucepan and sprinkle the agar agar flakes on top. Let stand for 10 minutes.

Place the saucepan over medium-high heat and bring to a boil. Reduce the heat to a simmer and cook, whisking frequently, for about 5 minutes, until the agar agar flakes are completely dissolved. Remove the pan from the heat and cool the mixture for 10 minutes.

Divide the lemon mixture among 4 wineglasses and refrigerate until set, about 1 hour.

MAKE THE ESPRESSO LAYER:

Combine the soy creamer, soy milk, cane juice sugar, and vanilla in a saucepan. Sprinkle the agar agar flakes on top and let stand for 10 minutes.

Place the saucepan over medium-high heat and bring to a boil. Reduce the heat to a simmer and cook, whisking frequently, for about 5 minutes, until the agar agar flakes are completely dissolved. Remove the pan from the heat and stir in the espresso. Cool the mixture for 15 minutes.

Slowly pour the mixture over the lemon layer in each wineglass. Chill for at least 2 hours before serving. Serve the desserts with a dollop of non-dairy whipped topping or Coconut Whipped Cream and a pinch of lemon zest.

CHOCOLATE-VANILLA TIRAMISU

It may not be classic, but this vegan version of tiramisu is just as creamy and delicious as the original. Make sure to allow time for chilling the dessert, as directed, so that the cookies soften up and soak in the flavors of the other ingredients.

SERVES 4

> ¼ cup (60 g/2 oz) soy milk
> ¼ cup (25 g/0.88 oz) tapioca starch
> ¼ cup (74 g/2.6 oz) brown rice syrup
> ¼ cup (54 g/1.9 oz) light brown sugar
> 1 teaspoon (4 g/0.14 oz) vanilla extract
> ⅛ teaspoon (0.37 g/0.01 oz) kosher salt
> 1 cup (232 g/8 oz) whippable soy topping,
>   such as Soya Too
> 16 (160 g/5.6 oz) Maple Pecan Sables (page 48) or any storebought
>   vegan shortbread cookies (I use Zest Brand Shortbread Sandies.
>   See Vegan Ingredient Sources, page 204)
> 2 tablespoons plus 2 teaspoons (11 g/0.4 oz)
>   grated vegan dark chocolate, such as Callebaut

Combine the soy milk and tapioca starch in a small saucepan and whisk together until combined and free of any lumps. Whisk in the brown rice syrup, brown sugar, and vanilla. Cook over medium heat, whisking constantly, until the mixture thickens considerably, about 2 minutes. Remove the pan from the heat and whisk in the salt. Set aside to cool for 15 minutes.

Using an electric stand or handheld mixer, whip the soy topping at high speed to medium peaks. Whisk the cooled brown sugar mixture vigorously to smooth it out, then add it to the whipped soy topping and whisk just until blended.

Crumble 2 of the vegan cookies into chunks and arrange them in the bottom of a parfait glass. Spoon about ½ cup of the tiramisu cream on top, then sprinkle with 1 teaspoon of grated chocolate. Repeat this layering once more with crumbled shortbread, cream, and chocolate. Repeat this process to make a total of 4 parfaits. Refrigerate for at least 4 hours before serving.

THE SAVVY DIVA

Place chocolate in the freezer for 10 minutes before grating it to prevent it from melting as you work (the heat from your hands can melt chocolate easily when you handle it directly).

VEGAN DIVAS CHOCOLATE MOUSSE

This is our most popular item at Vegan Divas, and with good reason. My aim with this recipe was to create the most *chocolaty* chocolate mousse ever, one that has the same silky texture as the classic version. The beautifully smooth quality of this mousse comes from a combination of high-quality chocolate, silky tofu, and just a touch of coconut oil. Fresh raspberries or a sprinkling of crunchy cacao nibs on top is the ideal finish for this indulgent dessert.

MAKES ABOUT 5 CUPS (1.2 KG/10.6 OZ), SERVING 8

2 cups (340 g/12 oz) vegan semisweet chocolate morsels

2 tablespoons (20 g/0.7 oz) liquid coconut oil

Two and a half 12.3-ounce (871-g/30.75-oz) packages extra-firm silken tofu

1 cup (154 g/5.4 oz) Sucanat

1½ tablespoons (18 g/0.63 oz) vanilla extract

¼ teaspoon plus ⅛ teaspoon (1.125 g/0.04 oz) kosher salt

Fresh raspberries or cacao nibs for garnish

Place the chocolate morsels and coconut oil in a heatproof bowl and set the bowl over a saucepan half filled with barely simmering water. Heat, stirring frequently, until the chocolate is melted and the mixture is smooth. Set aside to cool slightly.

Place the tofu, Sucanat, vanilla, and salt in the bowl of a food processor and process until very smooth, about 1 minute. With the processor running, add the melted chocolate to the tofu mixture through the feed tube. Continue to process until blended, occasionally scraping down the sides of the work bowl, about 1 minute. Scrape the mousse into a medium bowl, cover, and refrigerate for at least 5 hours or overnight before serving.

To serve, spoon or pipe the mousse into elegant serving glasses and garnish with fresh raspberries or cacao nibs.

HOST LIKE A DIVA

Because this mousse is so decadent and creamy, I like to top it with some fresh fruit when plating it to add a little tartness and acidity. Blueberries, raspberries, and strawberries all make an elegant crown for this mousse and add a bright pop of color.

CHOCOLATE BROWNIE MOUSSE PARFAIT

Here's an elegant dessert that features two of the most popular Vegan Divas items—our Chocolate Mousse and Brownies are much loved. The mousse is spooned into martini glasses, topped with a brownie, and then given a layer of chocolate glaze and a puffy cloud of soy milk foam. The sleek presentation makes the perfect ending for a dinner party or special event. You'll need either a whipped cream canister or a battery-operated milk frother to make the soy foam.

SERVES 8

SPECIAL EQUIPMENT:
Whipped cream canister loaded with one NO_2 charger or a milk frother
$1^1/_2$-inch round cookie or biscuit cutter

CHOCOLATE GLAZE:
$1/_3$ cup (85 g/3 oz) vegan bittersweet chocolate, finely chopped
$1/_4$ cup (60 g/2.1 oz) soy creamer

Vegan Divas Chocolate Mousse (page 117)
Vegan Divas Chocolate Brownies (page 46), baked in a 12-by-18-inch rimmed
    baking sheet

SOY MILK FOAM TOPPING:
$1/_2$ cup (121 g/4.3 oz) chilled soy milk

MAKE THE GLAZE:
Place the chocolate in a medium bowl and set aside.

Place the soy creamer in a small saucepan and bring to a boil. Pour the hot creamer over the chocolate and allow it to stand for 1 minute. Whisk the mixture until the chocolate is completely melted and the glaze is smooth. Cover the surface of the glaze with a piece of plastic wrap and let it cool for about 5 minutes before using.

MAKE THE FOAM TOPPING:

Place the chilled soy milk in a whipped cream canister loaded with an NO_2 charger. Refrigerate until ready to serve the desserts. (If you are using a milk frother, just froth the milk right before serving the desserts.)

ASSEMBLE THE DESSERTS:

Divide the chocolate mousse among 8 martini glasses. Using a $1^1/_2$-inch cookie or biscuit cutter, cut out 8 rounds from the chocolate brownies. Place one brownie round on top of the mousse in each glass. Pour a thin layer of chocolate glaze on top of the brownies and mousse. Dispense a mound of soy milk foam on top of each dessert and serve immediately.

CHOCOLATE LIÉGEOIS WITH TOFU-TAHINI ICE CREAM

Café liégeois is a classic European dessert made with layers of coffee ice cream, coffee, and whipped cream, and it's one of my favorites. Of course, I put my own spin on the classic, transforming it into a true vegan treat. Instead of using coffee as the primary flavor, though, I feature a tahini-flavored tofu ice cream and layer it with a rich chocolate glaze and soy whipped topping. The nutty sesame of the tahini pairs nicely with the dark chocolate—like a more sophisticated, subtle version of the classic combination of chocolate and peanut butter.

SERVES 6

SPECIAL EQUIPMENT:
Ice cream machine

TOFU-TAHINI ICE CREAM:
1 1/2 cups (349 g/12.3 oz) soft tofu
3/4 cup (181 g/6.4 oz) soy milk
1/2 cup plus 1 tablespoon (90 g/3.17 oz) vegetable oil
3/4 cup (150 g/5.3 oz) evaporated cane juice sugar
2 tablespoons (37 g/1.3 oz) tahini
3/4 tablespoon (9 g/0.3 oz) vanilla extract
Pinch of salt
2 3/4 tablespoons (25 g/0.88 oz) black sesame seeds

CHOCOLATE GLAZE:
1/3 cup (85 g/3 oz) vegan bittersweet chocolate, finely chopped
1/4 cup (60 g/2.1 oz) soy creamer

SOY WHIPPED TOPPING:
1 cup (232 g/8 oz) whippable soy topping, such as Soya Too

GARNISH:
Sliced almonds

MAKE THE ICE CREAM:

Combine all the ice cream ingredients except the sesame seeds in the bowl of a food processor and process until very smooth, about 1 1/2 minutes. Scrape the mixture into a medium bowl and stir in the sesame seeds.

Process the mixture in an ice cream machine according to the manufacturer's instructions. Transfer the ice cream to a covered container and freeze until ready to serve.

MAKE THE GLAZE:

Place the chocolate into a medium bowl and set aside.

Place the soy creamer in a small saucepan and bring to a boil. Pour the hot creamer over the chocolate and allow it to stand for 1 minute. Whisk the mixture until the chocolate is completely melted and the glaze is smooth. Cover the surface of the glaze with a piece of plastic wrap and let it cool for about 5 minutes before using.

MAKE THE WHIPPED TOPPING:

Using an electric stand or handheld mixer, whip the soy topping at high speed to medium peaks.

ASSEMBLE THE DESSERTS:

Place 2 scoops of the ice cream in the bottom of a wine or dessert glass. (If the ice cream has been frozen for more than 30 minutes, it will be very hard, so let it stand at room temperature for about 10 minutes before scooping.) Top with a layer (about 1/2 inch thick) of whipped topping, smoothing it into an even layer. Spoon a thin layer of chocolate glaze over the whipped topping. Repeat for the remaining 5 glasses. Garnish with a few sliced almonds and serve immediately.

HOST LIKE A DIVA

To make a flawless ice cream scoop, dip your scooper in hot water first, and dry it with a paper towel, leaving it a little bit damp. The hot metal will cut through the frozen ice cream more easily. Try to turn the scoop in one fluid motion until you have the desired amount, which will create a pretty rounded ball of ice cream.

PASSION FRUIT "WHITE CHOCOLATE" MOUSSE WITH FRESH STRAWBERRIES

I love the flavor of passion fruit—it's tart, but with a fresh, flowery back-note that is unlike any other fruit. Here, I add a passion fruit puree to a rich mousse made with cacao butter and tofu. I like to serve this delicious mousse with a topping of fresh sliced strawberries or other local berries.

SERVES 8

1 cup plus 3 tablespoons (200 g/7 oz) cacao butter (see Vegan Ingredient Sources, page 203)

1¼ cups (300 g/10.6 oz) passion fruit puree (see below)

3 tablespoons (22 g/0.8 oz) arrowroot

Two 12.3-ounce (697-g/24.6-oz) packages soft silken tofu, drained

1¼ cups plus 2 tablespoons (250 g/8.8 oz) Sucanat

⅛ teaspoon (0.8 g/0.03 oz) sea salt

½ teaspoon (2 g/0.07 oz) vanilla extract

1 pint (288 g/10 oz) fresh ripe strawberries, hulled and sliced, for serving

Place the cacao butter, passion fruit puree, and arrowroot in a small saucepan and cook over medium heat, stirring frequently, until the cocoa butter is melted and the mixture thickens slightly. Remove the pan from the heat.

Place the tofu, Sucanat, salt, and vanilla in the bowl of a food processor. Add the hot cocoa butter mixture and process until smooth and creamy, about 1½ minutes. Divide the mousse among 8 parfait glasses or bowls and refrigerate for at least 4 hours or overnight.

Before serving, top each serving of mousse with sliced strawberries.

THE SAVVY DIVA

Vitamin-rich passion fruit puree can be found in the frozen foods section at many grocery stores, or you can find jarred versions at some specialty food stores. If you have trouble locating it, you can also order it online from www.perfectpuree.com. For additional information, see Vegan Ingredient Sources, page 205.

SPICY ALMONDS

Infused with the subtle flavor of coconut oil, these salty, spicy almonds are ideal to serve at a cocktail party or as a midafternoon snack. You can use either sweet, smoked, or hot paprika, depending on how spicy you like them. They also make a great gift around the holidays—just pack them into a little tin and add a bow. What hostess wouldn't be happy to have this easy nibble on hand?

MAKES 3½ CUPS (497 G/17.5 OZ)

3½ cups (500 g/17.6 oz) whole unblanched almonds
2½ tablespoons (30 g/1 oz) liquid coconut oil
2 teaspoons (6 g/0.21 oz) kosher salt
½ teaspoon (2.5 g/0.08 oz) freshly ground black pepper
½ teaspoon (1 g/0.03 oz) chili powder
½ teaspoon (1 g/0.03 oz) paprika

Preheat the oven to 350°F. Line a baking sheet with a silicone baking mat or piece of parchment paper.

In a large bowl, toss together all the ingredients until the nuts are evenly coated. Scatter the nuts onto the baking sheet and bake until fragrant (a cut almond should be golden brown inside), about 8 minutes. Cool completely.

THE SAVVY DIVA

Unblanched almonds, also known as "raw" almonds, have been shelled but still retain the brown skin surrounding the nut. Raw almonds are a great source of fiber and nutrients, including vitamin E, manganese, magnesium, and tryptophan. They are also high in monounsaturated fats, which have been associated with lowering the risk of heart disease.

part six

BREAD
WINNERS

DELICIOUS JALAPEÑO CORNBREAD

Sweetened with a touch of maple syrup and spiced up with chopped jalapeño, this moist cornbread has a toasty corn flavor and slightly crunchy texture on the outside. And unlike most cornbread, it's also relatively low in fat and calories, yet rich in protein and fiber. Serve it as an accompaniment to soup or vegetable chili or on its own with a nice smear of buttery spread.

SERVES 9

1 cup (120 g/4.2 oz) white whole wheat flour
1 cup (137 g/4.8 oz) yellow cornmeal
1 tablespoon (12 g/0.4 oz) baking powder
1¼ teaspoons (4.25 g/0.15 oz) kosher salt
1 cup (242 g/8.5 oz) soy milk
¼ cup (60 g/2.1 oz) canned pumpkin puree
   (not pumpkin pie filling)
¼ cup (75 g/2.6 oz) maple syrup
1 tablespoon (10 g/0.35 oz) turbinado sugar
2 tablespoons (16 g/0.56 oz) finely chopped and
   seeded jalapeño pepper

Preheat the oven to 400°F. Grease an 8-inch square baking pan and set aside.

In a large bowl, whisk together the flour, cornmeal, baking powder, and salt until combined; set aside.

In another bowl, whisk together the soy milk, pumpkin puree, maple syrup, sugar, and jalapeño. Make a well in the center of the dry ingredients and pour the pumpkin mixture into the well; gradually stir it into the dry ingredients just until combined. Scrape the batter into the prepared pan and bake for 15 to 20 minutes, until a toothpick inserted into the center of the cornbread comes out clean. Cut into wedges and serve warm or at room temperature.

SPICY PUMPKIN BREAD

A combination of vegetable oil, coconut milk, and pumpkin puree makes this pumpkin bread wonderfully moist, while a generous amount of nutmeg, cloves, and cinnamon gives it a warm, spicy flavor. Well wrapped, these loaves will keep for at least a week.

MAKES TWO 8-BY-4-INCH LOAVES

1 cup (114 g/4 oz) chopped walnuts

3½ cups (448 g/15.8 oz) unbleached all-purpose flour

2½ cups (387 g/13.6 oz) Sucanat

2 teaspoons (10 g/0.35 oz) baking soda

1 teaspoon (9 g/0.3 oz) kosher salt

1 teaspoon (2 g/0.07 oz) ground nutmeg

1½ teaspoons (3 g/0.1 oz) ground cloves

1½ teaspoons (3 g/0.1 oz) ground cinnamon

2 cups (480 g/17 oz) canned pumpkin puree
   (not pumpkin pie filling)

1 cup (160 g/5.6 oz) vegetable oil

⅔ cup (160 g/5.6 oz) liquid coconut milk

⅔ cup (60 g/2.1 oz) unsweetened desiccated coconut

Preheat the oven to 350°F. Coat two 8-by-4-inch loaf pans with nonstick cooking spray.

Spread the walnuts in a single layer on an ungreased baking sheet. Toast in the oven for 8 to 10 minutes, tossing them once or twice, until lightly browned and fragrant. Set aside to cool.

In a large bowl, stir together the flour, Sucanat, baking soda, salt, nutmeg, cloves, and cinnamon. Make a well in the center of the dry ingredients. Add the pumpkin puree, vegetable oil, and coconut milk to the well and gradually stir the wet ingredients into the dry ones until all of the flour is absorbed and the mixture is blended (the batter will be thick). Fold in the coconut and toasted walnuts. Divide the batter evenly between the prepared pans. Bake for 55 to 65 minutes, until a toothpick inserted in the center of each loaf comes out clean. Remove the pans from the oven and place them on a wire cooling rack. Immediately cover the loaves tightly with a linen kitchen towel. Allow them to steam for 10 minutes.

Remove the towel and turn the loaves out onto a wire rack, right side up. Cover the loaves loosely with the towel and cool completely.

THE SAVVY DIVA

Pumpkin puree is not only delicious, it's also an excellent source of fiber and nutrition. It's low in fat and calories and contains vitamins A, K, C, and E, among others, and the nutrients potassium, calcium, and beta-carotene. If you want to make your own puree, purchase pumpkins in the fall, when they're in season.

EGGLESS WHOLE WHEAT
CHALLAH BREAD

My version of challah, the fluffy bread that's traditionally enriched with eggs, is made with whole wheat flour and, naturally, without the eggs. Yeast-based doughs require patience and can be tricky to master, but this impressive braided loaf, topped with a sprinkling of poppy seeds, is well worth the extra time and effort.

MAKES ONE 2-POUND LOAF, SERVING 12

2 tablespoons (19 g/0.7 oz) Sucanat

¼ cup (60 g/2.1 oz) lukewarm water (110°F)

2¼ teaspoons (7 g/0.25 oz) active dry yeast

2½ teaspoons (10 g/0.35 oz) egg replacer mixed
   with 1 cup (236 g/8.3 oz) warm water

2 teaspoons (6 g/0.21 oz) kosher salt

¼ cup (52 g/1.8 oz) sunflower oil,
   plus more for brushing the top of the loaf

2 cups (256 g/9 oz) unbleached all-purpose flour

1¾ to 2¼ cups (218 g/7.7 oz to 280 g/9.9 oz)
   whole wheat or organic whole wheat spelt flour

1 tablespoon (8 g/0.27 oz) poppy seeds

In a small bowl, stir the Sucanat into the warm water along with the yeast. Let stand for about 15 minutes, until the yeast is bubbly.

Pour the egg replacer mixture into a large bowl and stir in the dissolved yeast mixture along with the salt and oil. Gradually stir in the all-purpose flour and 1¾ cups of the whole wheat or spelt flour, ½ cup at a time, mixing until a dough forms. The dough should not be sticky; if it is, add just enough of the remaining flour until it is no longer wet. Transfer the dough to a floured work surface and knead for about 10 minutes, adding more flour as needed, until the dough is smooth and elastic. Place the dough in a clean bowl, cover with a dish towel, and let it rise in a warm place for 1½ hours, or until doubled in bulk.

Punch down the dough and divide it into 3 equal parts. Using your hands, roll each section into a 16-inch rope. Pinch the dough ropes together at one end and braid them together to form a loaf. Pinch the dough together at the other end of the loaf. Place the loaf on a baking sheet and loosely cover it with a dish towel. Allow it to rise until doubled in size, about 45 minutes. Meanwhile, preheat the oven to 350°F.

Brush the top of the loaf with sunflower oil and sprinkle with the poppy seeds. Bake for 25 to 30 minutes, until the bread is golden brown and sounds hollow when tapped with your finger. Cool on a wire rack.

TOMATO BASIL COUNTRY BREAD

This tomato-topped bread has all the flavors of bruschetta, one of my favorite appetizers, but it more closely resembles a casserole than a traditional bread loaf. This dish will only be as good as your tomatoes are, so make sure they are the best, and by that I mean perfectly ripe, juicy, and organic. The layer of toasted bread on the bottom of the dish soaks up all the tomato juices and olive oil, and when you take a bite you get the intoxicating flavor combination of tomato, basil, thyme, and garlic. Make this at the height of tomato season, and feel free to use heirloom varieties in assorted colors.

SERVES 6

    5 tablespoons (70 g/2.5 oz) extra-virgin olive oil
    1 loaf (340 g/12 oz) chewy (not fluffy) Italian-style bread
        (fresh or day-old)
    3 cloves (18 g/0.63 oz) garlic, finely chopped
    1/2 cup loosely packed (35 g/1.25 oz) fresh basil
    3 medium ripe juicy tomatoes, cored and sliced 1/2-inch-thick
    1/2 teaspoon (1.5 g/0.05 oz) kosher salt, or to taste
    1 tablespoon (0.5 g/0.017 oz) fresh thyme leaves

Preheat the oven to 400°F. Brush 1 tablespoon of the olive oil on the bottom of a 21/2-quart gratin dish (about 8 by 10 inches).

Cut the crust off the bread and slice it into rough pieces that are about 1 inch thick and 2 inches square. Fit the bread into a tight mosaic in the bottom of the dish to create a single layer of bread with no spaces (you may not use the entire loaf). Drizzle the bread with another 2 tablespoons of the oil and sprinkle with the garlic. Tear the basil leaves over the bread. Arrange the tomatoes in rows, overlapping them so they all fit. Drizzle with the remaining 2 tablespoons oil and sprinkle with the salt and thyme leaves. Bake for 25 to 30 minutes, until the underside of the bread is lightly toasted when you lift a corner to peek. Cool for about 10 minutes and serve warm, scooped from the dish with a large spoon.

WHOLE WHEAT BREAD

No-knead bread might be all the rage now, but I personally love the therapeutic process of kneading dough, especially when it yields a bread as flavorful as this one. Molasses and whole wheat flour combine to give this bread a beautiful brown color and earthy flavor. Use it for sandwiches, or toast it and serve it with jam for breakfast. This recipe can easily be doubled.

MAKES ONE 8½-BY-4½-INCH LOAF, SERVING 8

1¼ cups (295 g/10.4 oz) warm water
2 tablespoons (40 g/1.4 oz) unsulfured molasses
1 tablespoon (10 g/0.35 oz) active dry yeast
2½ to 3 cups (312 g/11 oz to 374 g/13.2 oz) whole wheat
   or organic whole wheat spelt flour
2 tablespoons (28 g/1 oz) sunflower oil
2 tablespoons (30 g/1 oz) soy milk
1½ teaspoons (4.5 g/0.15 oz) kosher salt
1½ teaspoons (3 g/0.1 oz) dried herb seasoning
   (any blend you prefer)
1 tablespoon (12 g/0.4 oz) egg replacer
   (not mixed with water)
1 tablespoon (8 g/0.28) bread flour (optional)

In a large bowl, combine the water, 1/2 tablespoon of the molasses, and the yeast. Allow it to stand for about 5 minutes, until the mixture is foamy.

Add 11/2 cups of the whole wheat or spelt flour and mix until well combined. Cover the bowl with a dish towel and set the bowl aside in a warm place for at least 20 minutes, or up to a day.

Coat the bottom and sides of an 81/2-by-41/2-inch loaf pan with nonstick cooking spray. Add the remaining 11/2 tablespoons of molasses, the sunflower oil, soy milk, salt, herb seasoning, egg replacer, and bread flour, if using, to the yeast and flour mixture and stir to combine. Gradually add the remaining 1 to 11/2 cups flour, adding just enough to form a dough that's not too sticky. Begin kneading the dough in the bowl, then turn the dough out onto a lightly floured work surface and knead for about 10 minutes, until it is smooth and elastic.

Shape the dough into a loaf and place, seam side down, in the prepared pan.

Cover the pan with a clean dish towel and set it in a warm place until the dough is doubled in size, about 1 hour.

Meanwhile, preheat the oven to 350°F.

Bake the loaf for 30 to 40 minutes, until it is golden brown and sounds hollow when tapped with a finger. Unmold the loaf and cool on a wire rack.

NANDA'S CINNAMON BUNS

These irresistible cinnamon buns were my favorite pastry as a child, and their fragrant scent always brings back a flood of happy memories for me. This is my grandmother's recipe, which I adapted to a vegan version, and it must be made in a bread machine. Make sure you spread the icing on the buns while they're warm so that it will melt in, giving them a sweet and oh-so-delicious gooiness.

MAKES 16 BUNS

SPECIAL EQUIPMENT:
Bread machine

YEAST DOUGH:
1/2 cup (118 g/4.16 oz) warm water
1/2 cup (121 g/4.7 oz) warm soy milk
1 teaspoon (3 g/0.1 oz) kosher salt
2/3 cup (133 g/4.7 oz) evaporated cane juice sugar
1 teaspoon (4 g/0.14 oz) egg replacer mixed with 2 tablespoons (30 g/1 oz) water
8 tablespoons (96 g/3.4 oz) vegan butter
4 cups (512 g/18 oz) unbleached all-purpose flour
1 tablespoon plus 1 teaspoon (12 g/0.42 oz) rapid-rise yeast

FILLING:
4 tablespoons (48 g/1.7 oz) vegan butter
1/4 cup evaporated cane juice sugar
1 teaspoon (2 g/0.07 oz) ground cinnamon

ICING:
1 cup (115 g/4 oz) vegan confectioners' sugar
1 tablespoon (14 g/0.5 oz) vegan butter, at room temperature
1 teaspoon (5 g/0.17 oz) soy milk
1/2 teaspoon (2 g/0.07 oz) vanilla extract

MAKE THE DOUGH:

Place all the ingredients for the dough, in the order listed, in the pan of a bread machine. Set the machine to the dough cycle and press the start button.

After the dough cycle is complete, let the dough remain in the bread machine to rise for 1 hour.

MAKE THE FILLING AND ASSEMBLE THE BUNS:

Coat a 9-by-13-inch baking pan with nonstick cooking spray. Transfer the dough to a lightly floured work surface and, using a rolling pin, roll it out into a 14-by-18-inch rectangle. Spread the dough with the butter and sprinkle with the cane juice sugar and cinnamon. Starting at a long end, roll the dough up jelly-roll style. Cut the roll into 16 equal slices. Arrange the slices in the prepared pan, cover with plastic wrap, and let rise for 45 minutes to 1 hour, until doubled in size (or refrigerate overnight and bring to room temperature before baking).

Meanwhile, preheat the oven to 375°F.

Bake the buns until lightly browned, 15 to 20 minutes. Remove from the oven and quickly make the icing by whisking together all the icing ingredients until smooth. Spread the icing over the warm buns and serve immediately.

HOST LIKE A DIVA

If you have a bread machine (and so many people do these days), these buns are the perfect treat to make for overnight guests. You can get up early, throw everything in the machine, and take a shower, then prepare the buns while everyone else is slowly making their way to the table. Trust me, nothing will make your guests happier than the smell of cinnamon buns wafting through the morning air!

Homemade "Buttermilk" Biscuits (pages 142–43)

HOMEMADE "BUTTERMILK" BISCUITS

These biscuits are made tender with the addition of homemade soy buttermilk, a mixture of soy milk and apple cider vinegar. The other trick to keeping them tender is to handle the dough gently, folding it rather than kneading it like bread dough. The biscuits are best eaten straight from the oven, as they become firmer as they cool.

MAKES 10 BISCUITS

SPECIAL EQUIPMENT:
2-inch round biscuit cutter

3/4 cup (181 g/6.4 oz) soy milk
1 tablespoon (15 g/0.5 oz) apple cider vinegar
2 cups (256 g/9 oz) unbleached all-purpose flour, sifted, plus more for dusting
1 tablespoon (15 g/0.5 oz) baking powder
3/4 teaspoon (2.25 g/0.08) kosher salt
1/4 cup (48 g/1.7 oz) vegan shortening

Preheat the oven to 400°F.

Pour the soy milk into a glass measuring cup and stir in the vinegar. Set aside for about 5 minutes, until curdled.

Place the sifted flour into a medium bowl and whisk in the baking powder and salt until well blended. Add the shortening, in chunks, and using a pastry blender or 2 knives, cut the shortening into the flour mixture until it resembles coarse crumbs. Add the soy milk and vinegar mixture one third at a time, mixing gently with a wooden spoon until a soft, shaggy dough forms. Turn the dough out onto a lightly floured work surface and dust it lightly with more flour. Using your hands, gently pat the dough so that it is about 1/2 inch thick. Fold the dough in half and pat it down again; repeat this process about 4 times, patting the dough out to a thickness of 1/2 inch the final time. Using a 2-inch round biscuit cutter, cut out 10 rounds from the dough (you can gather up the scraps, pat the dough down again, and cut out more rounds, but these biscuits will not be nearly as tender as the first batch). Place the biscuits on a baking sheet with their sides touching and bake for 12 to 16 minutes, until light golden brown on top. Serve warm.

THE SAVVY DIVA

If you don't have a biscuit or pastry cutter, you can use a round cookie cutter or even a drinking glass. Just make sure the edge cutting the dough is thin so that the dough is cut through easily.

GLAZED FRIED DOUGHNUTS

These yeast-based doughnuts are soft pillows of fried dough, coated with a thin, crackly glaze. Ground mace, which is the outer membrane of the nutmeg seed, adds a warm spicy note to this classic American treat. Glaze them while they're warm, let them set for a minute or two, then watch them disappear!

MAKES SIXTEEN 3-INCH DOUGHNUTS

SPECIAL EQUIPMENT:
Doughnut cutter

DOUGHNUTS:
2 1/4 teaspoons (7 g/0.25 oz) active dry yeast
1 cup (236 g/8.3 oz) lukewarm water (110°F)
1/4 cup (50 g/1.76 oz) vegan shortening
1/2 cup (100 g/3.5 oz) evaporated cane juice sugar
1/3 cup (80 g/2.8 oz) soy milk, warmed
1 tablespoon (12 g/0.42 oz) egg replacer mixed with
    1/4 cup (60 g/2.1 oz) warm water
4 cups (512 g/18 oz) unbleached all-purpose flour,
    plus more for dusting
1/2 teaspoon (1.5 g/0.05 oz) kosher salt
1/2 teaspoon (1 g/0.03 oz) ground mace
Canola oil for deep-frying

GLAZE:
2 cups (230 g/8.12 oz) vegan confectioners' sugar
1/2 cup (118 g/4.1 oz) hot water

Dissolve the yeast in 1/2 cup of the lukewarm water and allow it to stand for about 5 minutes, until it bubbles. Line a baking sheet with parchment paper.

In a small saucepan, bring the remaining 1/2 cup lukewarm water to a boil. Add the shortening and cane juice sugar and stir until they are dissolved. Pour the mixture into a medium bowl and allow it to cool to room temperature.

Stir the yeast mixture and soy milk into the shortening mixture. Stir in the egg replacer and water mixture along with 2 cups of the flour, the salt, and mace.

Add the remaining flour, a little at a time, mixing to form a soft dough. Knead the dough on a lightly floured surface until it is smooth, place it in a large bowl that has been sprayed with nonstick cooking spray, cover with a dish towel, and allow to rise for about 1 hour, until it has doubled in size.

Punch down the dough. On a lightly floured surface, using a floured rolling pin, roll the dough out gently until it is about 1/2 inch thick. Using a 2½-inch doughnut cutter, cut out as many rounds as possible from the dough and arrange them on the lined baking sheet (alternatively, you can use 2½-inch and 1-inch pastry cutters to do this). Cover the doughnuts loosely with a piece of plastic wrap that has been sprayed with nonstick cooking spray and allow them to rise for 1 hour in a warm place.

In a deep skillet or deep fryer, heat the canola oil to 370°F. Line another baking sheet with paper towels. In a shallow bowl, mix the confectioners' sugar with the hot water until blended and smooth. Set aside while you fry the doughnuts.

Fry a few doughnuts at a time, turning them over with a spider or slotted spoon, until they are golden brown all over, about 2 minutes. Place them on the paper towels to drain off the excess oil.

While the doughnuts are still hot, dip them in the glaze and place them onto a wire rack set over a parchment-lined baking sheet. Allow the glaze to set, about 2 minutes, then serve the doughnuts immediately.

BANANA BREAD

Brazil, my homeland, grows some of the best tropical fruit in the world, including 10 percent of the world's banana production (that's a lot of bananas). Bananas are a great source of potassium, vitamin B_6, folate, electrolytes, and soluble fiber, and, happily, they have a sweet, earthy flavor that is delicious. One of my favorite ways to eat them is in this easy quick bread, which is made with whole wheat flour and maple syrup. The addition of applesauce and coconut oil makes the bread moist—just be sure to use extra-ripe bananas, as they will give off more liquid and have a more intense flavor than less ripe ones.

MAKES ONE 9-BY-5-INCH LOAF, SERVING 10

1 cup (128 g/4.5 oz) unbleached all-purpose flour
1 cup (125 g/4.4 oz) whole wheat flour
1 teaspoon (5 g/0.17 oz) baking powder
1 teaspoon (5 g/0.17 oz) baking soda
1/4 teaspoon (0.75 g/0.03 oz) kosher salt
2 medium (290 g/10.2 oz) extra-ripe bananas
   (about 3/4 cup mashed banana)
2 tablespoons (28 g/1 oz) liquid coconut oil
1/2 cup (150 g/5.3 oz) maple syrup
1/2 cup (121 g/4.3 oz) unsweetened applesauce

Preheat the oven to 375°F. Coat the bottom and sides of a 9-by-5-inch loaf pan with nonstick cooking spray.

In a large bowl, whisk together the flours, baking powder, baking soda, and salt until blended. Set aside.

In a small bowl, mash the bananas with a fork until they are very mushy, then stir in the coconut oil, maple syrup, and applesauce until well blended. Stir the banana mixture into the flour mixture, just until combined. Scrape the batter into the prepared pan and bake for 25 to 30 minutes, until a toothpick inserted into the center of the loaf comes out clean. Cool in the pan on a wire rack for 15 minutes, then unmold the loaf and cool completely on the rack.

CHOCOLATE CHIP PEANUT BUTTER BANANA BREAD

If you like banana bread, you will love this indulgent recipe, which features a chocolate–peanut butter–banana combo that will knock your socks off. Make sure you use high-quality vegan chocolate morsels—it will make all the difference in the flavor.

MAKES ONE 9-BY-5-INCH LOAF, SERVING 10

3 cups (384 g/13.5 oz) unbleached all-purpose flour

1 tablespoon (15 g/0.5 oz) baking powder

1½ teaspoons (3 g/0.1 oz) ground cinnamon

1 teaspoon (2 g/0.07 oz) freshly grated nutmeg

1¼ teaspoons (3.75 g/0.13 oz) kosher salt

3 large extra-ripe bananas

¾ cup (180 g/6.3 oz) natural peanut butter (smooth or crunchy)

¾ cup (181 g/6.4 oz) soy milk

½ cup (108 g/3.8 oz) liquid coconut oil

½ cup (150 g/5.3 oz) maple syrup

1 tablespoon plus 1 teaspoon (16 g/0.56 oz) vanilla extract

¾ cup (127 g/4.5 oz) vegan semisweet chocolate morsels

Preheat the oven to 325°F. Coat a 9-by-5-inch loaf pan with nonstick cooking spray.

In a large bowl, sift together the flour, baking powder, cinnamon, and nutmeg. Whisk in the salt and set aside.

In another large bowl, mash the bananas with a fork until they are pureed. Add the peanut butter and mix vigorously with the fork until blended. Whisk in the soy milk, coconut oil, maple syrup, and vanilla until well blended. Gradually stir the dry ingredients into the wet ingredients, mixing just until blended. Fold in the chocolate morsels. Scrape the batter into the prepared loaf pan and bake for about 1 hour, until golden brown and a toothpick inserted into the center of the cake comes out clean. Cool the cake in the pan on a wire rack for 15 minutes, then invert the loaf onto the rack and cool completely.

SPICY SWEET POTATO SODA BREAD

This dense bread will fill your kitchen with the wonderful fragrance of orange and cloves. The unexpected addition of chili powder gives it a subtle kick—I love the combination of sweet and spicy. This makes a great St. Patrick's Day stand-in for traditional Irish soda bread. Serve it with vegan butter and orange marmalade for a breakfast treat.

MAKES ONE ROUND LOAF

1 cup (242 g/8.5 oz) soy milk

1 tablespoon (15 g/0.5 oz) apple cider vinegar

1/2 cup (113 g/4 oz) mashed cooked sweet potato

2 cups (250 g/8.8 oz) whole wheat pastry flour

3/4 teaspoon (3.75 g/0.13 oz) baking soda

1/4 teaspoon (1.6 g/0.05 oz) salt

1 tablespoon (13 g/0.45 oz) Sucanat

3/4 teaspoon (1.5 g/0.05 oz) chili powder

1/4 teaspoon (0.5 g/0.017 oz) ground cloves

1/4 teaspoon (0.5 g/0.017 oz) ground cinnamon (optional)

2 tablespoons (20 g/0.68 oz) diced candied orange rind

1/3 cup (33 g/1.16 oz) chopped pecans

1/3 cup (53 g/1.8 oz) dried cranberries

Preheat the oven to 400°F. Coat a baking sheet with nonstick cooking spray.

In a medium bowl, whisk together the soy milk, vinegar, and mashed sweet potato. Set aside.

Combine the flour, baking soda, salt, Sucanat, and spices in a large mixing bowl. Add the liquid ingredients to the flour mixture and stir until just combined. Using your hands, mix in the candied orange rind, pecans, and dried cranberries.

Transfer the dough to a lightly floured work surface and form it into a round loaf. Place the loaf on the prepared baking sheet and score the top a few times with a sharp knife. Bake the loaf for 30 to 40 minutes, covering it with parchment paper after 20 minutes if it is browning too quickly, until the loaf sounds hollow when tapped with your finger. Cool on a wire rack before slicing and serving. Store in a paper bag at room temperature for up to 3 days.

part seven

SOUPS, SANDWICHES, SALADS, AND SUCH

SMOKY TOMATO-BEAN SOUP

The base of this nourishing soup is made from lots of fresh, ripe tomatoes, which are an excellent source of lycopene, vitamin C, and potassium. Smoked tempeh and paprika add a smoky-sweet flavor to the soup, while white cannellini beans add protein and fiber. Serve this with myJalapeño Cornbread (page 128)—it's a match made in heaven.

SERVES 6 (MAKES 2 QUARTS)

2 tablespoons (14 g/0.5 oz) olive oil
1/2 cup (113 g/4 oz) chopped smoked tempeh
1 medium onion, finely diced
3 tablespoons (6 g/0.21 oz) chopped sage leaves
3 cloves garlic, finely chopped
1 tablespoon (6 g/0.21 oz) sweet smoked paprika (see Vegan Ingredient
    Sources, page 204)
About 12 medium ripe tomatoes, peeled, seeded, and diced (see Note)
1 tablespoon (9 g/0.3 oz) kosher salt
2 tablespoons (4 g/0.14 oz) coarsely chopped sweet marjoram
One 15 1/2-ounce (439-g) can cannellini or other white beans, drained and rinsed
Salt and freshly ground black pepper

Heat the olive oil in a large saucepan over medium heat, then add the chopped tempeh and cook, stirring frequently, until it turns crisp, about 4 minutes. Add the onion, sage, garlic, and paprika and continue to cook, stirring occasionally, until the onion softens, about 4 minutes. Stir in the tomatoes and salt, partially cover, reduce the heat to medium-low, and simmer for 30 minutes, or until the tomatoes have released their liquid and the mixture is soupy.

Stir in the marjoram and beans and cook for 5 more minutes, or until the beans are heated through. Season with salt if you like (the smoked tempeh is already a little salty) and pepper. Keep the soup over low heat until ready to serve.

Note: To peel the tomatoes, half fill a medium saucepan with water and bring the water to a boil over high heat. Using a paring knife, cut a small X in the pointed end of each tomato. Add 3 tomatoes at a time to the boiling water and, once the water returns to a boil, boil them for 20 to 30 seconds. Using a slotted spoon, transfer the tomatoes to a bowl of ice water. Repeat with the remaining tomatoes. To seed the tomatoes, cut each one in quarters and scoop out and discard the seeds with your fingers.

SPICED RED LENTIL AND COCONUT MILK SOUP

Red lentils have a sweet, slightly nutty flavor and a beautiful orange color. Because they cook relatively quickly, they are an ideal ingredient to feature in a pureed soup such as this. Accented with Indian spices, this lentil soup is further enriched with coconut milk, which gives it a silky texture. A final drizzle of coconut milk and a sprinkling of cumin seeds make an elegant garnish.

SERVES 6 (MAKES 2 QUARTS)

2 medium onions, finely chopped
2 cloves garlic, crushed
4 medium tomatoes, cored and coarsely chopped
2 medium carrots (198 g/7 oz) chopped
1½ teaspoons (3 g/0.1 oz) ground turmeric
1 tablespoon (6 g/0.21 oz) ground cumin
6 cardamom pods
½ cinnamon stick
1 cup (214 g/7.5 oz) red lentils
3¾ cups (885 g/31.2 oz) water
1½ cups plus 2 tablespoons (400 g/14 oz) coconut milk
1 tablespoon (15 g/0.5 oz) fresh lime juice
Kosher salt and freshly ground black pepper
Cumin seeds for garnish

In a large saucepan, combine the onions, garlic, tomatoes, carrots, turmeric, cumin, cardamom pods, cinnamon, and lentils. Add the water and bring to a boil over high heat. Reduce the heat to medium-low so that the soup is just simmering, cover, and simmer gently for about 20 minutes, until the lentils are soft.

Remove and discard the cardamom pods (they are easy to find because they swell up when cooked) and cinnamon stick. Process the mixture in a blender or food processor to a smooth puree. Press the soup through a fine-mesh sieve (this step is optional, but it will give the soup an ultrasmooth texture), then return it to a clean saucepan.

Reserve about 2 tablespoons of the coconut milk to garnish the soup and add the remainder to the pan along with the lime juice. Stir well. Season with salt and pepper.

Reheat the soup gently over medium-low heat without boiling. Ladle into heated bowls, swirl about 1 teaspoon of the reserved coconut milk on the surface of each serving, and garnish with a few cumin seeds.

THE SAVVY DIVA

I like to mix lentils with grains such as rice for a dish that offers a complete protein. Aside from being a good source of protein and fiber, red lentils are also rich in vitamins and minerals, including folate (which your body needs to produce iron), vitamin A, potassium, phosphorus, and magnesium. Brown and green lentils are also delicious and offer many health benefits.

CREAMY CARROT AND MUSHROOM SOUP

Made from dried sea kelp, *dashi kombu* is used in Japanese cooking to make a flavorful base for soups. A homemade kombu stock and pureed carrots give this delicious soup a slightly sweet, complex flavor, while soy milk adds a creamy texture. Sliced mushrooms and a garnish of finely chopped carrot tops contribute an earthy accent to this sophisticated soup.

SERVES 4 (MAKES ABOUT 1 QUART)

KOMBU STOCK:
1²/₃ cups (393 g/13.87 oz) water
One 4-inch piece (3 g/0.1 oz) dried kombu
1 tablespoon (16 g/0.5 oz) miso paste

SOUP:
1 tablespoon (9 g/0.31 oz) kosher salt
3 medium (210 g/7.4 oz) carrots,
    peeled and cut into ¹/₂-inch pieces
1²/₃ cups (402 g/14.2 oz) soy milk
8 small button or shiitake mushrooms, sliced
1²/₃ cups (400 g/14.1 oz) kombu stock
2 tablespoons (30 g/1 oz) sake or dry white wine
Finely chopped carrot leaves or parsley for garnish

MAKE THE KOMBU STOCK:

Place the water and kombu in a small saucepan and allow to soak for 2 hours.

Place the pan over medium heat and stir in the miso paste. Cook, stirring occasionally, just until the miso paste is dissolved; remove the stock from the heat before it begins to boil and discard the kombu.

MAKE THE SOUP:

Half fill a medium saucepan with water and add 1 teaspoon of the salt. Bring the water to a boil over high heat and add the carrots. Boil for 15 minutes, or until very soft. Drain the carrots and put them in the bowl of a food processer or blender with the soy milk. Process until smooth, about 30 seconds.

To the saucepan containing the kombu stock, add the mushrooms, the remaining 2 tea-spoons of salt, and the sake or wine and cook over medium heat until the stock just begins to boil. Reduce the heat to medium-low and simmer for 5 minutes, or until the mushrooms shrink slightly and are cooked through. Stir in the carrot puree and bring to a boil, stirring occasionally. Remove the pan from the heat and serve hot, garnished with the carrot leaves or parsley.

The Savvy Diva

Stored in the drawer of your refrigerator, carrots have a lifespan of at least 10 days. Just make sure to separate them from apples, tomatoes, avocados, and other fruits and vegetables that produce ethylene gas, which will cause them to become bitter. To revive limp carrots, soak them in ice water for 5 minutes.

CHILLED SWEET CORN SOUP WITH RED PEPPER COULIS AND CROUTONS

This recipe was inspired by an amazing corn soup that Chef Philippe Bertineau used to make at Payard Bistro in New York. The flavorful corn stock base is made from simmered corn husks, while sweet corn kernels give the pureed soup its full body. Rosemary and thyme add a woodsy accent, and a garlicky roasted red pepper coulis makes a bright accompaniment. Make this soup when summer corn is at its peak in July and August.

SERVES 6 (MAKES 2 QUARTS)

SPECIAL EQUIPMENT:
Plastic squeeze bottle
Cheesecloth

RED PEPPER COULIS:
2 medium (340 g/12 oz) red bell peppers
3 tablespoons (42 g/1.5 oz) extra-virgin olive oil
2 cloves garlic, peeled and cut in half
4 sprigs thyme
1 teaspoon (4 g/0.14 oz) evaporated cane juice sugar
Salt and freshly ground black pepper

SOUP:
12 ears yellow corn, husked
3 tablespoons (42 g/3 oz) olive oil
1 medium (227 g/8 oz) yellow onion, chopped
1 bay leaf
3 sprigs thyme
1 sprig rosemary
Salt and freshly ground white pepper

CROUTONS:
1 slice white bread
2 tablespoons (28 g/1 oz) vegan butter

MAKE THE COULIS:

Preheat the oven to 400°F.

Cut the red peppers in half and remove the stems and seeds. Rub the pepper halves all over with 1 tablespoon of the olive oil and place them on a baking sheet, cut side up. Place 1 thyme sprig and 1/2 garlic clove on top of each half and roast for 25 to 30 minutes, until the skin of the peppers begins to wrinkle and the peppers are completely cooked through. Place the roasted peppers in a bowl along with the garlic and thyme, cover with plastic wrap, and cool completely.

Using your fingers, peel away the skin of the peppers and remove any seeds you may have missed earlier. Discard the garlic and thyme. Put the peppers into a blender and puree with the remaining 2 tablespoons of olive oil and the sugar until completely smooth. Pass the mixture through a fine-mesh sieve and season with salt and pepper. Pour the coulis into a plastic squeeze bottle and refrigerate until ready to use.

MAKE THE SOUP:

Remove the kernels from the ears of corn by holding each ear vertically in a large bowl and, using a chef's knife, slicing off the kernels into the bowl. Once you've removed all the kernels, cut or break each cob into 2 or 3 pieces and place them into a large (5- or 6-quart) pot. Cover the cobs with water (about 10 cups) and bring the water to a boil over high heat. Reduce the heat to medium-low and simmer for 30 minutes to make a corn stock. Strain the stock, discarding the corn cobs. Measure out 6 cups of the stock for the soup (discard the rest or cover and refrigerate it for another use).

Heat 2 tablespoons of the olive oil in a large saucepan over medium-high heat, add the onion and cook until softened, about 4 minutes. Add all but 1/4 cup of the corn kernels (these will be used to garnish the soup) to the saucepan and cook until tender, stirring frequently, about 8 minutes. Add the corn stock, bay leaf, thyme, and rosemary and bring to a boil. Season with salt and pepper. Reduce the heat to medium-low and simmer the soup for 20 minutes. Cool for 15 minutes.

Remove and discard the bay leaf and herb sprigs and puree the soup in batches in a blender until smooth, then pass it through a fine-mesh sieve into a large stainless steel bowl. Set the bowl in another large bowl that is filled one third of the way with ice water and allow to stand, stirring occasionally, until chilled, about 20 minutes.

Meanwhile, heat the remaining 1 tablespoon of olive oil in a small skillet over medium-high heat and add the reserved corn. Cook, stirring occasionally, until the corn is tender, about 5 minutes. Set aside to cool.

MAKE THE CROUTONS:

Trim the crust away from the slice of bread and cut it into 1/4-inch cubes. Melt the butter in a small skillet over medium-high heat and add the bread cubes. Cook, tossing frequently, until the bread is golden brown. Remove the pan from the heat and allow the croutons to cool.

TO SERVE:

Ladle the chilled soup into 6 bowls and place a spoonful of the reserved corn in the centers. Sprinkle a few croutons in the center and squeeze dots of the coulis on the surface of the soup.

ROASTED KABOCHA SQUASH WITH PEANUT SAUCE

The kabocha squash, also known as the Japanese pumpkin, has a squat shape, a deep green skin, and a wonderful sweet flavor that's a cross between a sweet potato and a pumpkin. I love to roast wedges of the yellow-orange flesh and serve it with a thick, salty peanut sauce as an appetizer. If you prefer a thinner sauce, simply thin it out with 2 to 3 tablespoons of water. Regular pumpkin or other varieties of squash can also be swapped in for kabocha squash in a pinch.

SERVES 4

14 ounces (397 g) kabocha squash, seeds and stringy fibers
    removed and sliced into thin (1/4-inch) wedges
Liquid coconut oil for brushing
1/4 cup plus 2 tablespoons (90 g/3.17 oz) smooth natural
    peanut butter
2 tablespoons (32 g/1.12 oz) white miso paste
2 tablespoons (30 g/1 oz) sake or white wine
3 tablespoons (47 g/1.6 oz) fresh lemon juice
2 tablespoons (30 g/1 oz) soy sauce

Preheat the oven to 325°F.

Brush the squash wedges with coconut oil and arrange them on a rimmed baking sheet. Bake until golden on both sides, 40 to 45 minutes.

To make the sauce, in a small bowl whisk together the peanut butter, miso paste, sake or wine, lemon juice, and soy sauce until well blended.

Divide the roasted squash wedges among 4 serving plates and serve with the peanut sauce.

HOST LIKE A DIVA

When I make a dish that requires a sauce, I like to serve it on the side. Everyone has their own preferences—some guests like to drizzle the sauce over their entree, while others prefer to spoon a little sauce on the side. I serve sauces in a gravy boat or a ramekin with a small ladle.

PARTY BRUSCHETTA

The combination of fresh, flavorful toppings and crisp whole wheat toast makes this easy appetizer the life of any party. You can serve the "bruschetta" already assembled, or just put out a platter of toasted bread and small bowls of the toppings to let guests make their own combinations. If you don't have time to make bread, you can pick up a whole wheat loaf or whole wheat pita bread at the store. To ensure the best texture, make the toppings within a few hours of serving.

SERVES 15

TOAST RECTANGLES:
Whole Wheat Bread (page 136)

GUACAMOLE TOPPING:
1 medium Hass avocado, peeled and cut
    into ¼-inch cubes
1½ tablespoons (9 g/0.31 oz) chopped fresh cilantro
1 tablespoon plus 1 teaspoon (12 g/0.42 oz) minced white onion
2 teaspoons (30 g/1 oz) fresh lime juice
½ teaspoon (3.2 g/0.1 oz) sea salt
Freshly ground black pepper to taste

TOMATO TOPPING:
4 medium tomatoes, cored and cut
    into ¼-inch cubes
4 large tomatillos, husks removed, seeded, and cut
    into ¼-inch cubes
1 tablespoon plus 1 teaspoon (12 g/0.42 oz)
    minced red onion
2 teaspoons (10 g/0.34 oz) fresh lime juice
1 tablespoon plus 1 teaspoon (17.2 g/0.6 oz)
    extra-virgin olive oil
8 tiny mustard green leaves
Sea salt to taste

CORN AND BEAN TOPPING:

1 cup (283 g/10 oz) cooked black beans

1½ cups (246 g/8.7 oz) corn kernels

1 tablespoon (15 g/0.52 oz) fresh lime juice

2 tablespoons plus 2 teaspoons (34 g/1.2 oz) extra-virgin olive oil

12 fresh cilantro leaves, chopped

Sea salt to taste

ASSEMBLY:

Chopped chives or basil for garnish

MAKE THE TOAST RECTANGLES:

Preheat the oven to 325°F. Cut the bread into ½-inch slices and then cut fifteen 2-by-2 ½-inch rectangles from the slices (5 rectangles for each topping). Place the rectangles on a baking sheet and bake them for 10 minutes, until lightly toasted.

MAKE THE GUACAMOLE TOPPING:

Combine all the ingredients in a bowl and stir to mix. Do not overmix—the mixture should be somewhat chunky.

MAKE THE TOMATO TOPPING:

Combine all the ingredients in a bowl and toss to mix.

MAKE THE CORN AND BEAN TOPPING:

Combine all the ingredients in a bowl and toss to mix.

ASSEMBLY:

When the toppings are ready, divide each one among 5 toast rectangles. Garnish with chopped chives or basil and serve immediately.

TOMATO AND AVOCADO SALAD

This is one of my favorite summer salads—rich chunks of avocado, ripe tomato cubes, and lots of peppery arugula, dressed with a light lemon and cilantro vinaigrette. Make sure you wash and spin the arugula well, particularly if you buy it from a farmers' market—it can have a lot of grit on it.

SERVES 2

2 medium tomatoes, cored and cut into 1/2-inch cubes
1 medium ripe Haas avocado
2 cups packed (71 g/2.5 oz) arugula leaves, washed and spun dry
3 tablespoons (47 g/1.6 oz) fresh lemon juice
1/3 cup (72 g/2.5 oz) extra-virgin olive oil
1 cup loosely packed (24 g/0.84 oz) fresh cilantro leaves, chopped
Sea salt and freshly ground black pepper

Place the cubed tomatoes in a medium bowl. Cut the avocado in half lengthwise, cutting around the pit to separate the halves. Firmly (but carefully!) strike the pit with a chef's knife and then twist to remove it. Using a spoon, scoop the avocado flesh from each half and cut into 1/2-inch cubes. Add the avocado to the tomato in the bowl along with the arugula.

In a medium bowl, whisk the lemon juice while gradually adding the olive oil in a slow stream. Whisk in the cilantro and season with salt and pepper. Pour the dressing over the salad and toss gently to combine. Check the seasoning, adding more salt and pepper if necessary.

THE SAVVY DIVA

Haas avocados have a distinctively bumpy green skin that turns purple-black when ripe. A perfectly ripe avocado should also yield to pressure when gently squeezed. Haas avocados are known for their creamy texture and, luckily, are available year-round. Avocados are a good source of many nutrients, including potassium, vitamin E, and folic acid.

WATERMELON TOMATO SALAD

Watermelon and tomato may sound like an odd pairing, but these two fruits complement each other perfectly, especially in this refreshing summer salad. Cubes of tofu absorb the juices of the fruits and the dressing, and chopped basil and red onion add some zing to the mix. Take the trouble to seek out sherry vinegar for the vinaigrette—it has a deep, complex flavor that's worth every extra penny you'll spend for it. Add some fresh arugula or spinach to give some color if you wish to.

SERVES 4

1/3 cup (80 g/2.8 oz) sherry vinegar
1/4 cup (60 g/2.1 oz) soy sauce
1/2 cup (109 g/3.8 oz) extra-virgin olive oil
1 medium (227 g/8 oz) red onion, chopped
2 large (454 g/1 lb) organic tomatoes, cored and cut into 1/2-inch cubes
1/2 cup (113 g/4 oz) extra-firm silken tofu, drained and patted dry
1/4 small seedless watermelon, rind removed and cut into 1/2-inch cubes (about 6 cups)
6 basil leaves, chopped

To make the dressing, in a medium bowl, whisk together the vinegar and soy sauce. Slowly whisk in the olive oil until blended. Whisk in the chopped onions. Add the tomatoes to the bowl and toss to coat. Allow the tomatoes to marinate at room temperature for 30 minutes to 1 hour.

Meanwhile, preheat the oven to 325°F.

Place the tofu on a baking sheet and bake for 30 minutes, turning it over halfway through baking. Set the tofu aside to cool for 15 minutes.

When the tofu has cooled enough to handle, cut it into 1/2-inch cubes. Toss the tofu cubes with the tomatoes. Add the watermelon and basil and toss to combine. Serve immediately.

When choosing a watermelon, look for a pale yellow patch on one side, which tells you that the melon has been left on the vine longer and will be sweeter than others. Store watermelon in the refrigerator for up to a week.

VEGETABLE SUSHI ROLLS

Making sushi rolls is a great way to serve a variety of brightly colored vegetables. Though you can choose your favorites, here I feature carrots and avocado, with a little dill pickle for contrast. You can cook the rice and prepare the carrots and pickles in advance (hold off on the avocado, as it will discolor), but assemble the rolls shortly before serving for the freshest flavor and best texture.

MAKES 4 ROLLS

SPECIAL EQUIPMENT:
Bamboo sushi rolling mat

SUSHI RICE (MAKES 5¾ CUPS, 1069 G/37.7 OZ):
1½ cups (192 g/6.7 oz) uncooked Japanese sushi rice
2 cups (152 g/5.3 oz) water
One 4-inch piece dried kombu
¼ cup (60 g/2.1 oz) rice vinegar
2 tablespoons (25 g/0.88 oz) evaporated cane juice sugar
1 tablespoon (9 g/0.31 oz) kosher salt

SUSHI ROLLS:
1 medium carrot, peeled
½ medium ripe Haas avocado, pitted and peeled
½ medium dill pickle
4 nori seaweed sheets (about 8 inches square)
Pickled ginger slices for garnish
Soy sauce for serving

MAKE THE SUSHI RICE:
Rinse the rice well and allow it to drain for 30 minutes.

Place the rice and water into a medium saucepan over high heat. Bring to a boil, un-covered. Once it begins to boil, reduce the heat to the lowest setting, add the kombu, and cover. Cook for 15 minutes, then remove from the heat and let stand, covered, for 10 minutes.

In a small, microwave-safe cup, combine the vinegar, sugar, and salt and heat in the microwave on high power for 30 to 45 seconds, until the sugar is dissolved. Discard the kombu and transfer the rice to a large glass bowl. Add the vinegar mixture and fold thoroughly to combine and coat each grain of rice with the mixture. Allow to cool to room temperature before using.

ASSEMBLE THE ROLLS:

Cut the carrot into rectangles that measure 4 inches long and 1/4 inch wide. Fill a small saucepan halfway with water and bring to a boil. Add the carrot strips and boil for 6 to 7 minutes, until cooked through. Cut the avocado and pickle into pieces that also measure 4 inches long and 1/4 inch wide. Lay out a sushi rolling mat on a work surface so that the slats are horizontal to you, and place a sheet of nori on top, shiny side down. Carefully spread about 1 cup of the sushi rice over the nori, leaving a border of 3/4 inch around the edges of the sheet. Lay 2 pieces each of carrot, pickle, and avocado horizontally across the bottom edge of the rice (the one that is closest to you). Starting at this edge, pick up the rolling mat and nori together and roll up the sushi tightly, jelly-roll style (don't roll up the mat with the nori!—just use it as a guide to form the roll). Once the sushi is rolled, squeeze the rolling mat firmly to shape the roll into a solid cylindrical shape. Press both ends to make sure that no sushi rice falls out. Remove the rolling mat. Repeat to form a total of 4 rolls. Run the blade of a sharp knife under hot water and cut the sushi logs into 1/2-inch pieces (warm the knife in hot water before each cut). Serve the rolls with pickled ginger and soy sauce.

THE SAVVY DIVA

Japanese sushi rice is a short-grain rice that gets sticky when cooked. The texture and stickiness are ideal for sushi rolls because they help to keep the rolls together.

KALE CHIPS

Kale is a leafy green that has a *lot* going for it in the nutrition department: it's high in beta carotene, vitamin K, vitamin C, and calcium, and it's also a great source of indole-3-carbinol, which boosts DNA repair in cells, as well as carotenoids. Here's one of my favorite ways to eat this superfood—as a delicious snack chip. These are so addictive you'll find it hard to believe they're good for you! If you like, you can add some heat by sprinkling them with a little chili powder or a few red pepper flakes.

MAKES ABOUT 4½ CUPS

> 1 bunch curly kale, center stems removed and each leaf torn
>   into 4 pieces (for a total of 6 cups)
> 2 tablespoons (42 g/1.5 oz) olive oil
> 1 tablespoon (15 g/0.5 oz) fresh lemon juice
> ½ teaspoon (3.5 g/0.12 oz) sea salt
> 3 tablespoons (12 g/0.42 oz) nutritional yeast

Position 3 racks near the center of the oven and preheat the oven to 175°F (or whatever your oven's lowest setting is). Line 3 baking sheets with parchment paper or silicone baking mats.

Place the kale pieces in a large bowl. Make sure the leaves are dry; if they aren't, dry them well with paper towels. In a small bowl, combine the olive oil, lemon juice, and salt. Drizzle the mixture over the leaves and toss the leaves until they are evenly coated. Sprinkle the nutritional yeast on top, then toss the leaves again to coat. Spread the leaves out onto the prepared baking sheets, trying not to overlap them at all, and let them dry in the oven for 45 minutes. Turn the oven off and let the kale pieces continue to dry in the oven for another 30 to 45 minutes, until they are crispy.

THE SAVVY DIVA

Store kale greens in a partially opened plastic bag with a damp paper towel inside to provide some moisture. Make sure to eat the kale within a few days of purchasing, as the leaves turn limp quickly. Wash kale greens well and cut out the tough stalk from each of the leaves with a knife before cooking.

BLUE POTATO-KALE SALAD

Blue potatoes have a striking, purplish-blue color, which, when combined with vibrant red kale leaves, make a very colorful potato salad. Caramelized onions and fresh rosemary add a sophisticated flavor to this lovely salad, and a dressing made from olive oil, lemon juice, and soy sauce is light and tangy. You can substitute sweet potatoes for the blue potatoes if you prefer.

SERVES 4

10 baby purple potatoes, scrubbed and patted dry
3/4 cup plus 2 tablespoons (190 g/6.7 oz) extra-virgin olive oil
3/4 teaspoon (2.25 g/0.07 oz) kosher salt
2 teaspoons (3 g/0.1 oz) chopped rosemary leaves
1 large white onion, chopped
3 tablespoons (47 g/1.6 oz) fresh lemon juice
2 tablespoons (30 g/1 oz) soy sauce
3 large leaves red kale, stemmed and chopped

Preheat the oven to 325°F.

Place the potatoes in a large bowl and drizzle with 1/4 cup of the olive oil. Sprinkle with the salt and rosemary and toss to combine. Arrange the potatoes on a rimmed baking sheet and roast, tossing them occasionally, until tender, about 40 minutes. Set the potatoes aside to cool.

Heat 2 tablespoons of the remaining olive oil in a medium skillet over medium-high heat. Add the onion, reduce the heat to medium-low, and cook, stirring occasionally, until the onions have turned a caramelized golden brown, about 40 minutes. Remove the pan from the heat and let the onions cool.

To make the dressing, in a small bowl, whisk together the lemon juice and soy sauce. Gradually whisk in the remaining 1/2 cup of olive oil.

Cut the potatoes into 1/2-inch slices and place them in a bowl. Add the caramelized onion, kale, and dressing and toss to combine.

GRILLED VEGETABLE SALAD WITH BALSAMIC DRESSING

Grilling adds a new level of caramelized flavor to a variety of vegetables, particularly in this delicious vegetable salad. Here I use a combination of eggplants, tomatoes, bell peppers, and zucchini, but feel free to choose your own favorites, or use what's on hand. This salad, along with a side of couscous or rice, is hearty enough to serve as a main dish.

SERVES 4

SPECIAL EQUIPMENT:
Propane or charcoal grill

4 small eggplants
4 medium tomatoes
4 medium red bell peppers
1 medium green bell pepper
2 medium zucchinis
2 tablespoons (28 g/1 oz) extra-virgin olive oil, plus extra for brushing the grill
¼ cup (45 g/1.6 oz) pitted kalamata or niçoise olives
1 clove garlic, minced
3 tablespoons (30 g/1 oz) capers
2 tablespoons (30 g/1 oz) balsamic vinegar
1½ teaspoons (6 g/0.22 oz) evaporated cane juice sugar
Kosher salt and freshly ground black pepper

Trim the eggplants, cut each one in half lengthwise, and then cut each half lengthwise into 3 pieces. Core each tomato, cut in half through the stem end, and cut each tomato half into 3 wedges. Cut each red and green bell pepper in half lengthwise, remove the stems, seeds, and membranes, and cut each half into 3 long strips. Trim the ends off the zucchinis and cut each one lengthwise into very thin (⅛-inch) strips.

Preheat a grill and brush it with olive oil so that the vegetables don't stick. Grill the vegetables for 3 to 4 minutes on each side, until they are lightly charred and softened. Transfer to a baking sheet or platter and cool completely.

Toss the cooled vegetables in a salad bowl with the olives, garlic, and capers. In a small bowl, whisk together the vinegar and sugar. Very gradually whisk in the 2 tablespoons of olive oil until blended. Pour the dressing over the vegetables and toss well to coat. Season with salt and pepper. Serve at room temperature.

PISSALADIÈRE WITH VEGETABLES AND OLIVES

Half tart, half pizza, the pissaladière is a classic recipe from the Provence region of France. My version features a mélange of multicolored vegetables—zucchini, fennel, eggplant, and onions—on top of an olive oil–enriched crust. It's ideal as a main dish for dinner, alongside a green salad. It's a great recipe for entertaining. Leave out the cooked veggies and each guest can choose their own topping.

SERVES 4

DOUGH:

2 cups (250 g/8.8 oz) unbleached all-purpose flour

1/4 teaspoon (0.75 g/0.026 oz) kosher salt

Pinch freshly ground black pepper

1/8 teaspoon (0.4 g/0.014 oz) turbinado sugar

4 1/4 tablespoons (60 g/2.1 oz) vegan butter, cut into 1/2-inch cubes

5 tablespoons (74 g/2.6 oz) water

6 tablespoons (84 g/3 oz) extra-virgin olive oil

TOPPING:

6 tablespoons (84 g/3 oz) extra-virgin olive oil,
    plus more for brushing on the baking sheet

4 medium yellow onions, thinly sliced

1 medium zucchini, thinly sliced

Kosher salt and freshly ground black pepper

1 small eggplant, thinly sliced

1 bulb fennel, thinly sliced

12 pitted niçoise or kalamata olives, halved

Leaves from 2 sprigs fresh thyme

MAKE THE DOUGH:

Place the flour in a large bowl and stir in the salt, pepper, and sugar. Add the butter cubes to the flour and, using your fingers, mix them in until they are evenly distributed and the mixture is crumbly. Make a well in the center and add the water and olive oil. Gradually stir the liquid ingredients into the flour until the mixture is evenly combined and forms a dough. Shape the dough into a disk, wrap in plastic wrap, and allow to rest at room temperature for 30 minutes while you prepare the topping.

PREPARE THE TOPPING:

In a large skillet, heat 5 tablespoons of the olive oil over medium-high heat and add the onion slices. Cook, stirring frequently, for about 5 minutes, until softened. Sprinkle the zucchini slices with salt and pepper and add them to the skillet. Cook for about 5 minutes, stirring frequently, until the onions begin to caramelize and the zucchini starts to turn translucent. Add the eggplant and fennel slices, reduce the heat to medium, and cook for about 10 minutes, stirring frequently so that the heat reaches the uncooked vegetables, until the vegetables are just softened. Remove the skillet from the heat and cool until you are ready to use the topping.

ASSEMBLE THE PISSALADIÈRE:

Preheat the oven to 325°F. Brush a 9-by-13-inch baking pan with olive oil.

On a lightly floured work surface, using a rolling pin, gently roll the dough out to a rectangle that roughly measures 9 by 13 inches. Roll the dough up onto the rolling pin and fit it into the baking pan. Using a table knife, cut the excess dough from around the edge of the pan and fit the trimmings into any empty spaces in the pan. Continue until the bottom of the pan is covered with an even layer of dough.

Arrange the cooked vegetables in an even layer on top of the dough. Scatter the olives and thyme leaves on top and bake for 35 to 40 minutes, until the dough base is golden brown and cooked through and the vegetables are lightly browned. Cut into squares and serve immediately.

THE SAVVY DIVA

Eggplants are available year-round. I enjoy them roasted, baked, pureed into a silky, smooth dip, or even grilled. They are a great source of fiber, which helps to regulate blood sugar and keeps cholesterol levels low (I eat eggplant when I'm trying to lose weight!). Look for eggplants with smooth, glossy skin and a green cap. Small eggplants generally are sweeter than large ones. They can be stored in the crisper drawer of your refrigerator for up to 5 days.

Walnut Pâté Apple Sandwiches (page 182)

WALNUT PÂTÉ APPLE SANDWICHES

This delicious sandwich features a high-protein pâté made from white beans and toasted walnuts, crunchy slices of green apple, and whole-grain bread. The pâté is similar to hummus—both are flavored with lemon juice and garlic—and, like hummus, it can also stand on its own as a dip, served with crudités or crackers. Ripe Anjou pears also work well in this sandwich in place of the apples.

MAKES 8 SANDWICHES

WALNUT PÂTÉ:
1 cup (100 g/3.5 oz) walnut halves
One 15.5-ounce (439-g) can cannellini beans,
    rinsed and drained
2 tablespoons (30 g/1 oz) fresh lemon juice
1 to 2 cloves garlic, minced
2 teaspoons (9 g/0.32 oz) extra-virgin olive oil
Salt and freshly ground black pepper

SANDWICHES:
16 slices whole-grain bread
4 large jarred roasted red bell peppers,
    rinsed, drained, and halved
2 large organic Granny Smith apples, peeled, cored,
    and thinly sliced vertically
2 cups packed (40 g/1.4 oz) baby spinach,
    rinsed and spun dry

MAKE THE PÂTÉ:
Preheat the oven to 350°F.

Spread the walnuts on a baking sheet and toast for 7 to 10 minutes, shaking the pan occasionally, until lightly browned and fragrant. Cool for 10 minutes.

Transfer the toasted walnuts to the bowl of a food processor. Add the beans, lemon juice, garlic, olive oil, and 1/4 cup water. Purée until smooth, about 45 seconds. Season with salt and pepper.

ASSEMBLE THE SANDWICHES:

Spread each of 8 bread slices with 1 to 2 tablespoons of the walnut pâté. Top each with a red bell pepper half, 2 apple slices, and 1/4 cup baby spinach. Spread the remaining 8 bread slices with 1 tablespoon of the walnut pâté. Place on top of the sandwiches and serve.

THE SAVVY DIVA

The average sandwich doesn't exactly have a stellar nutritional profile; usually it amounts to little more than a heavy dose of carbs and fat. But this sandwich—packed with calcium-rich walnuts and white beans, which are loaded with antioxidants, fiber, and protein—is a true power lunch!

NORI-WRAPPED TEMPEH WITH KALE

In the outdoor food markets in Indonesia, tempeh is sold wrapped in banana leaves. I copied that tradition in this recipe, but use nori instead of banana leaves as my wrapping. I sauté the shiny packages in a little oil and then serve them on a bed of wilted kale with a drizzle of tangy caper sauce on top. Delicious!

SERVES 4

Two 8-ounce (227-g) packages organic soy tempeh

8 sheets nori

6 tablespoons (78 g/2.7 oz) extra-virgin olive oil

1/3 cup (53 g/1.86 oz) capers

1 small bunch kale, stems removed, leaves trimmed, washed, spun dry, and cut into thin strips

3 tablespoons (47 g/1.6 oz) fresh lemon juice

Sea salt

MAKE THE TEMPEH:

Cut each block of tempeh in half crosswise to form a total of 4 squares, then cut each into 2 triangles. Wrap each triangle of tempeh in a sheet of nori to form a package.

Heat 1 tablespoon of the olive oil in a large skillet over medium heat until hot. Reduce the heat to low and add the tempeh packages to the skillet, seam side down. Cook for 10 minutes on each side, or until heated through. Remove the skillet from the heat. Transfer the tempeh packages to a plate and loosely cover with parchment paper to keep warm.

In a small bowl, stir 1/4 cup of the remaining olive oil with the capers and set aside.

MAKE THE KALE AND ASSEMBLE THE DISH:

Heat the remaining 1 tablespoon of olive oil in the skillet over medium heat. Add the kale to the skillet and cook for about 5 minutes, tossing frequently, until the leaves are wilted. Drizzle the lemon juice over the kale and sprinkle with a little salt. Divide the kale among 4 plates and place a tempeh package on each plate. Spoon some of the caper sauce on top of the tempeh and serve immediately.

HOST LIKE A DIVA

I use nori sheets in many dishes when I'm entertaining. The striking color and texture really adds polish to a dish, and shows your guests that you've taken the time to assemble a special "package" just for them. I also use protein-rich nori in rice dishes, quiche, pasta, and sandwiches, simply because it's so good for you!

VEGETABLE SKEWERS WITH BASIL COUSCOUS

Whenever I go to a traditional American barbecue, I am always surprised by how much meat is served! I suspect most people don't realize how delicious grilled vegetables can be, especially when they are marinated before grilling. These vegetable skewers are brushed with a lime-balsamic vinaigrette, which gives them a bright flavor that complements the fluffy basil couscous. They are bound to be the hit of your next barbecue. Feel free to get creative and add cubes of your favorite protein, such as tofu or tempeh, to the skewers as well.

SERVES 6

SPECIAL EQUIPMENT:
Propane or charcoal grill
18 bamboo skewers

3 medium zucchinis, cut into 1/2-inch cubes
4 small eggplants, cut into 1/2-inch cubes
12 medium mushrooms, cut in half
2 red bell peppers, cut into 1/2-inch squares
1 cup (250 g/8.8 oz) tempeh or extra-firm tofu,
    cut into 1/2-inch cubes (optional)
1/3 cup (80 g/2.8 oz) fresh lime juice
1/4 cup (60 g/2.1 oz) balsamic vinegar
2 cloves garlic, minced
2/3 cup (148 g/5.2 oz) extra-virgin olive oil
1 1/2 cups (283 g/10 oz) couscous
2 cups water
1 tablespoon (6 g/0.21 oz) lime zest
1/2 teaspoon (1.5 g/0.05 oz) kosher salt
5 tablespoons (19 g/0.67 oz) chopped fresh basil
2 limes, quartered
Salt and freshly ground black pepper

Soak the bamboo skewers in a shallow pan of water for 15 minutes so that they don't burn on the grill.

Thread the vegetables and tempeh onto the skewers, alternating each type in an even pattern (you will have more zucchini and eggplant than other vegetables). Place them in a shallow baking dish and set aside.

In a medium bowl, whisk together the lime juice, vinegar, and garlic. Gradually whisk in 1/2 cup plus 1 tablespoon of the olive oil until blended. Pour the mixture over the vegetable skewers and allow them to marinate at room temperature for 15 minutes.

Preheat the grill.

Meanwhile, prepare the couscous. In a small saucepan, bring 2 cups of water to a boil and stir in the couscous, lime zest, and salt. Cover and allow to stand for 5 minutes, or until the water is absorbed. Add the remaining 1 tablespoon plus 2 teaspoons of olive oil and the basil and stir with a fork until blended. Cover and set aside while you grill the vegetable skewers.

Grill the skewers for 4 to 5 minutes on each side, until the vegetables are lightly charred and cooked through. Sprinkle with salt and pepper. Serve 3 vegetable skewers on each plate with some couscous and 2 lime quarters.

The Savvy Diva

Couscous is a type of pasta that is typically made from semolina flour, though you can also find varieties made with whole wheat flour, barley, or ground millet. Because it doesn't have a strong flavor of its own, it makes a great base for meals with richly spiced sauces or other flavorful components.

SAUTÉED TOFU WITH ASIAN MUSHROOMS AND HARICOTS VERTS

This hearty tofu and vegetable dish comes together quickly in a wok or skillet, and is served with fragrant jasmine rice. The vegetables are cooked just until they're crisp-tender, so they still have a little bite. *Haricots verts*—long, thin French green beans—are more tender and flavorful than regular green beans, so do seek them out if you can—you will notice the difference.

SERVES 4

2½ cups (600 g/21.16 oz) extra-firm silken tofu,
    drained and cut into ¾-inch cubes
2¼ cups (531 g/18.7 oz) water
1½ cups (250 g/8.8 oz) jasmine rice
¾ teaspoon (2.25 g/0.07 oz) kosher salt
¼ cup (56 g/2 oz) peanut or grapeseed oil
2 cloves garlic, minced
2¾ cups (400 g/14.1 oz) sliced shiitake or
    whole enoki mushrooms
⅛ small head (100 g/3.5 oz) red cabbage,
    thinly sliced (about 1 cup)
3 cups (336 g/11.85 oz) haricots verts, trimmed
1 tablespoon water
¼ cup (60 g/2.1 oz) low-sodium soy sauce

To press some of the water out of the tofu, place the cubes on a plate with a lip and place another plate on top of them. Put a small saucepan (or other object with a similar weight) on top of the plate to weigh it down, and let stand for about 20 minutes, occasionally draining the water from the plate.

Pour the 2¼ cups of water into another small saucepan and bring to a boil over high heat. Stir in the rice and salt, cover, and reduce the heat to low. Simmer for 15 minutes, or until all the water is absorbed. While the rice is cooking, prepare the sautéed tofu and vegetables.

Heat 2 tablespoons of the oil in a wok or large skillet over medium-high heat and add the pressed tofu cubes. Sauté, stirring constantly, for 3 to 5 minutes, until golden brown. Transfer the tofu to a plate.

Add the remaining 2 tablespoons of oil to the wok and add the garlic, mushrooms, cabbage, haricots verts, and 1 tablespoon of water. Cook, stirring, for 2 to 3 minutes, until the vegetables are crisp-tender. Return the tofu cubes to the pan, add the soy sauce, and cook for another minute, or until the tofu is heated through. Serve the vegetables and tofu with the jasmine rice.

THE SAVVY DIVA

A good-quality wok is a kitchen essential for me. The surface of a wok heats up quickly, is larger than a traditional pan, and distributes heat evenly, so it allows you to cook a lot of food quickly. I use mine to cook veggies with garlic, chiles, onions, and other aromatics.

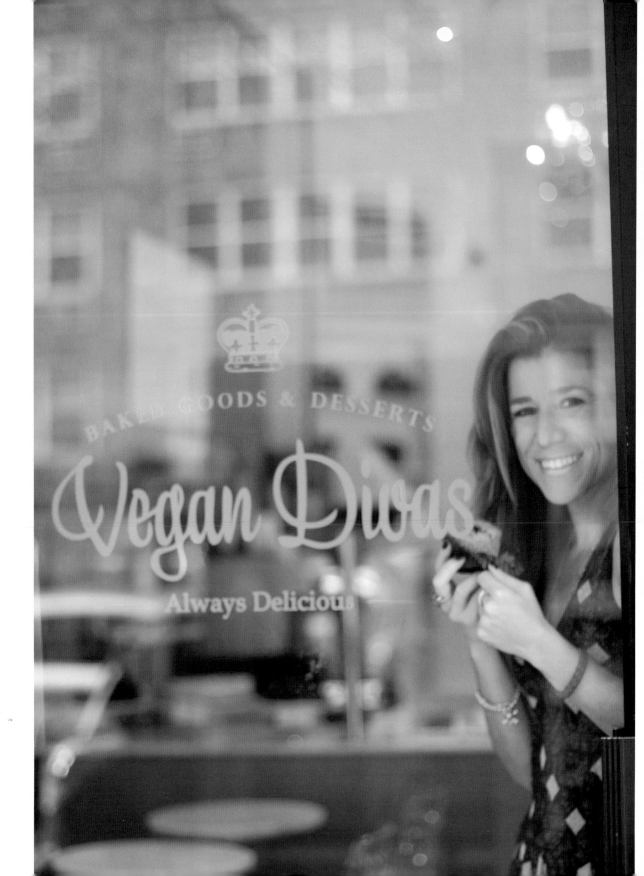

MACARONI AND "CHEESE"

I like to serve this vegan mac and cheese in small ramekins at a cocktail party. It's always the first thing to disappear! The nutritional yeast gives this dish a delicious "cheesy" flavor, and the combination of rice milk and tamari gives it a rich, creamy texture. Your dairy-free friends will beg you for this recipe!

MAKES SIX 1-CUP SERVINGS OR TWELVE ½-CUP SERVINGS (680 G/8 OZ)

3 cups (340 g/12 oz) small shell or penne pasta
1 clove garlic
1 cup (64 g/2.25 oz) nutritional yeast
1 teaspoon (5 g/0.17 oz) miso paste (any kind)
1 teaspoon (3 g/0.1 oz) paprika
¼ cup (60 g/2.1 oz) tamari
1 cup (242 g/8.5 oz) rice milk
⅔ cup (145 g/5.1 oz) extra-virgin olive oil
Salt and pepper to taste
Chopped chives for garnish

Cook the pasta according to the package directions until al dente (in other words, it shouldn't be soft—it should still have some bite to it).

In a blender or food processor, combine the garlic, nutritional yeast, miso, and paprika, and process until the garlic is finely chopped. Slowly add the tamari, rice milk, and olive oil and blend until creamy.

Transfer the sauce to a large saucepan and place over medium heat, stirring frequently, until heated through. Add the cooked pasta and toss to coat. Serve the macaroni in either six 8-oz ramekins (as a main course) or twelve 4-oz ramekins (as an appetizer or hors d'oeuvre), garnished with chopped chives.

part eight

VEGAN DIVA
BASICS

BASIC VEGAN PIE CRUST

Though premade vegan pie crusts are readily available, nothing beats a homemade one. This versatile pie crust is tender and flavorful, and the dough is very forgiving—even if you're not an expert with dough, this recipe comes out well every time!

**MAKES ONE 9-INCH PIE CRUST
(PLUS ENOUGH DOUGH FOR A LATTICE TOP)**

1 cup (227 g/8 oz) vegan butter, chilled and
   cut into 1/2-inch cubes
2 1/4 cups (288 g/10.15 oz) unbleached all-purpose flour
1 teaspoon (3 g/0.1 oz) kosher salt
1 tablespoon (12 g/0.4 oz) evaporated
   cane juice sugar
1/3 to 1/2 cup (78 g/2.75 oz to 118 g/4.16 oz)
   ice-cold water

Place the butter and flour in the freezer for at least 30 minutes.

Place the chilled flour, the salt, and the cane juice sugar in the bowl of a food processor and pulse to combine. Scatter the butter cubes over the flour and pulse until the mixture forms coarse crumbs. With the motor running, add 1/3 cup of the water through the feed tube and mix until the dough just starts to form a ball on the blade. Add more water, 1 tablespoon at a time, if the dough seems too dry. Transfer the dough to a lightly floured work surface and shape it into a disk. Wrap tightly in plastic wrap and freeze the dough for at least 1 hour before rolling it out.

Place the unwrapped dough disk on a lightly dusted work surface. Using a rolling pin, roll the dough out into a circle that is 1/8 inch thick, lifting and rotating the dough often while dusting the work surface and dough lightly with flour as necessary. Roll the dough up on the rolling pin and unroll it over a 9-inch pie pan. Gently press the dough onto the bottom and up the sides of the pan. Trim the edges of the dough with scissors, leaving about 3/4 inch of overhang. Tuck the overhanging dough underneath itself, pressing it onto the rim of the pan. Flute the edges by pinching the dough from the outside in a V shape with your thumb and index finger while poking the center of the shape with the index finger of your other hand from the inside. Lightly prick the bottom of the dough with a fork at 1/2-inch intervals. Refrigerate the dough in the pan for 20 minutes to firm it up (if your pie recipe calls for an unbaked pie crust, stop here; if you need a prebaked crust, continue to the next step).

Preheat the oven to 350°F.

Right before baking, line the dough with parchment paper and cover with pie weights or dried beans. Place the pie pan on a baking sheet and bake for 20 minutes. Carefully lift the parchment paper (along with the weights) out of the pie pan and bake the crust for 10 to 15 minutes longer, until golden brown. Transfer the pie pan to a wire rack and cool completely.

GINGERSNAP PIE CRUST

This spicy gingersnap crumb crust is super-quick to make and serves as a perfect shell for pumpkin pie or cheesecake. It's also a great solution for a quick dessert if you suddenly find yourself with guests on your hands—just mash up some day-old cookies and mix together! My Vegan Chocolate Chip Cookies (page 58) or Maple Pecan Sable Cookies (page 48) are also delicious in this crust.

MAKES ONE 9-INCH PIE CRUST

1¾ cups (198 g/7 oz) Spicy Gingersnaps (page 67)
   or store-bought vegan gingersnaps, crumbled
¼ cup (54 g/1.9 oz) packed light brown sugar
¼ teaspoon (0.75 g/0.026 oz) kosher salt
5 tablespoons (70 g/2.5 oz) vegan butter,
   melted

Preheat the oven to 350°F.

In a large bowl, whisk together the gingersnap crumbs, brown sugar, and salt. Add the melted butter and stir until the mixture is well combined. Press the crumb mixture into a 9-inch pie plate, evenly covering the bottom and sides. Place the pie plate on a baking sheet and bake until the crust is fragrant and set, about 8 minutes. Transfer the pie crust to a wire rack and cool completely before filling.

COCONUT WHIPPED CREAM

This topping is made by whipping the chilled fat that rises to the top of a can of coconut milk. Use it in place of dairy whipped cream or whipped topping in any variety of desserts. I like to use it in recipes like Pumpkin Pie (page 100) and Espresso-Lemon Panna Cotta (page 112). It also makes a great topping for vegan ice cream sundaes, quick homemade desserts, pancakes, or even coffee drinks!

MAKES ABOUT 1½ CUPS (174 G/6.13 OZ)

Two 14-ounce (794-g/28-oz) cans full-fat coconut milk
¼ cup (28 g/1 oz) vegan confectioners' sugar
¾ teaspoon (3 g/0.1 oz) vanilla extract

Refrigerate the cans of coconut milk (unopened) for at least 8 hours.

Five minutes before you are ready to whip the cream, place the bowl of an electric mixer in the freezer.

Flip the cans upside down, remove the bottoms with a can opener, and carefully pour the liquid coconut milk into a container (you only need the solidified coconut fat for this recipe; reserve the liquid coconut milk to use in smoothies). Scoop the solidified coconut fat into the chilled bowl and add the confectioners' sugar and vanilla. Using the whisk attachment, whip at high speed until the cream forms soft peaks, about 3 minutes. Use the whipped cream immediately or refrigerate for up to 4 hours before using.

VEGAN CREAM CHEESE FROSTING

This creamy non-dairy cream cheese frosting comes together in a snap, and is great for icing layer cakes like my Spicy Carrot Cake (page 81). Try spreading a dollop onto molasses cookies or gingersnaps for a truly decadent cookie treat.

MAKES ABOUT 4½ CUPS (1 KG/35.3 OZ)

15 tablespoons (212 g/7.5 oz) vegan butter
1 cup (226 g/8 oz) non-hydrogenated vegetable shortening
1½ teaspoons (6 g/0.21 oz) vanilla extract
2 cups (454 g/1 lb) vegan cream cheese
2 cups vegan confectioners' sugar, sifted

In the bowl of an electric mixer fitted with the paddle attachment, beat the butter, shortening, and vanilla at medium speed until blended, about 2 minutes. Scrape down the sides of the bowl with a rubber spatula, then beat on high speed until light and fluffy, about 2 minutes. Add the cream cheese and mix at medium-low speed just until combined (overmixing the frosting at this point will make it grainy). Gradually add the confectioners' sugar and mix at medium-low speed until well blended and creamy, about 2 minutes. Cover the bowl and refrigerate the frosting for at least 2 hours before using.

TOASTED NUTS AND COCONUT

Toasting brings out the full flavor of nuts. I love to add toasted nuts to a variety of dishes both sweet and savory. Not only do they provide extra flavor and texture, they also add a dose of heart-healthy protein to your meal. Make sure to watch the nuts carefully as they toast—they can burn easily.

NUTS:

Preheat the oven to 350°F.

Spread the nuts in a single layer on a half-sheet pan and toast for 5 to 12 minutes (time will vary depending on the nut variety; see the guide below), shaking the pan once or twice during baking, until they are golden (if they have skins, look beneath the skin) and fragrant. Transfer them to a plate to cool. The nuts can be stored in an airtight container for up to a day.

TOASTING TIMES:

Slivered or sliced almonds: 5 to 10 minutes
Whole almonds: 10 to 15 minutes
Walnuts and pecans: 5 to 10 minutes
Hazelnuts: 8 to 12 minutes
Pistachios: 5 to 7 minutes

COCONUT:

I use unsweetened desiccated (dried) coconut flakes in my recipes. Because coconut burns easily, I always toast it in a skillet over medium heat, tossing constantly, just until it turns golden.

The Savvy Diva

I am a huge fan of nuts—they're my number-one on-the-go snack. Almonds, walnuts, cashews, and pecans are all flavorful and so good for you. They are a rich source of minerals like manganese (which helps to fight those wrinkle-causing free radicals!), potassium, calcium, iron, magnesium, and zinc. When purchasing nuts, look for dry roasted or raw varieties.

HOMEMADE VANILLA ALMOND MILK

If you have the time, it's definitely worth it to make your own almond milk. Not only will you save money in the long run, but the flavor of fresh almond milk is much richer and nuttier than what's available at the grocery store. You'll need a nut milk bag to filter the milk; these are available at health food stores and from a number of sources online.

MAKES 3½ CUPS (847 G/30 OZ)

SPECIAL EQUIPMENT:
Nut milk bag

1 cup (120 g/4.2 oz) raw almonds
3½ cups (826 g/29.13 oz) filtered water
2 to 4 pitted Medjool dates, to taste
1 vanilla bean, chopped, or ¾ teaspoon (3 g/0.1 oz) vanilla extract
Small pinch of sea salt
1 tablespoon (18 g/0.63 oz) agave syrup (optional)

Place the almonds in a medium bowl and cover with water. Allow the nuts to soak overnight at room temperature.

Drain and rinse the almonds and place them in a blender with the filtered water, pitted dates, and chopped vanilla bean or extract. Blend on high speed for 1 to 1½ minutes, until the nuts are finely ground.

Place a nut milk bag over a large bowl and slowly pour the almond milk mixture into the bag. Slowly squeeze the bottom of the bag to release the milk. This process will take around 5 minutes to extract all the milk.

Rinse out the blender and pour the milk back in. Add the pinch of sea salt and the agave, if you're using it, and blend on low to combine.

Store the milk in a covered glass jar in the refrigerator for up to 5 days. Shake before using because it will separate on standing.

SAUCES

During the summer or when I just want to detox a little, I try to eat raw vegetables for lunch and dinner. Other than preparing them in a salad, one of my favorite ways to enjoy fresh vegetables is by making little veggie "wraps." I cut up some of my favorites—tomatoes, cauliflower, broccoli, cucumber, carrots, radishes, and watercress—and pile them onto a leaf of endive or iceberg lettuce to create a carb-free wrap. To make things a little more interesting, I'll whip up a sauce to use as a topping or dip for my wrap. These are a few of my favorites.

PEANUT LIME SAUCE

MAKES 1 CUP (240 G/8.4 OZ)

1 to 2 garlic cloves
2 tablespoons (25 g/0.88 oz) sesame oil
¼ cup (60 g/2.1 oz) natural peanut butter
1 tablespoon (15 g/0.5 oz) peeled and
    roughly chopped fresh gingerroot
3 tablespoons (45 g/1.6 oz) fresh lime juice
2 tablespoons (30 g/ 1 oz) low-sodium tamari
1 teaspoon (6 g/0.21 oz) agave syrup
1 to 3 teaspoons (15 g/0.5 oz to 45 g/1.6 oz) water,
    as needed to thin out sauce
½ medium carrot, chopped

In a small food processor or blender, process the sauce ingredients until smooth. You can adjust the taste with more agave, tamari, oil, or lime juice and adjust the consistency by adding more water.

"CHEESY" GARLIC SAUCE

MAKES 2 CUPS (480 G/16.8 OZ)

5 to 6 cloves garlic
¼ cup plus 2 tablespoons (90 g/3.17 oz) apple cider vinegar
¼ cup plus 2 tablespoons (90 g/3.17 oz) low-sodium tamari
¼ cup plus 2 tablespoons (88 g/3.12 oz) water
1 cup (64 g/2.2 oz) nutritional yeast
¼ cup (53 g/1.86 oz) extra-virgin olive oil or grapeseed oil

Combine the garlic, vinegar, tamari, and water in a blender and process until smooth, about 1 minute. Add the yeast and mix until combined. With the blender running, gradually add the oil in a slow stream. Store the sauce in a covered jar in the refrigerator for up to 3 weeks.

DIJON BASIL VINAIGRETTE

MAKES 1½ CUPS (360 G/12.7 OZ)

⅓ cup (80 g/2.8 oz) fresh lime juice
2 cloves garlic, minced and pressed
1 tablespoon (15 g/0.5 oz) low-sodium tamari
1 tablespoon (15 g/0.5 oz) Dijon mustard
¼ teaspoon (0.5 g/0.017 oz) black pepper
1 teaspoon (2 g/0.07 oz) finely chopped fresh parsley
2 teaspoons (4 g/0.14 oz) finely chopped fresh basil
1 teaspoon (4 g/0.14 oz) evaporated cane juice sugar
¾ cup (161 g/5.6 oz) extra-virgin olive oil

Whisk together all the ingredients except the olive oil until blended. Gradually add the oil in a slow stream while whisking until combined. Store the sauce in a covered jar in the refrigerator for up to a week.

VEGAN INGREDIENT SOURCES

I always try to choose the freshest ingredients, and, whenever possible, purchase organic and local. I buy produce that is in season so that its flavor and texture will be at their peak. At Vegan Divas, all of our ingredients are also kosher. Here's a list of some of my favorite brands.

NON-DAIRY MILKS

ALMOND MILK
Almond Breeze: *www.almondbreeze.com*

HAZELNUT AND OAT MILK
Pacific Foods: *www.pacificfoods.com*

RICE MILK
Rice Dream: *www.tastethedream.com*
Pacific Foods: *www.pacificfoods.com*
Westbrae: *www.westbrae.com*

SOY MILK
Eden Soy: *www.edenfoods.com*
Westsoy: *www.westsoy.biz*
Pacific Foods: *www.pacificfoods.com*
Wildwood Organics:
   www.wildwoodfoods.com

TOFU

House Foods: *www.house-foods.com*
Mori Nu (this is the brand we use at
   Vegan Divas): *www.morinu.com*
Nasoya: *www.nasoya.com*

NON-DAIRY BUTTER

Earth Balance: *www.earthbalance.net*
Spectrum: *www.spectrumorganics.com*

SUGARS AND OTHER SWEETENERS

SUCANAT, TURBINADO, AND ORGANIC COCONUT PALM SUGAR; ORGANIC MAPLE SYRUP; AGAVE NECTAR; MOLASSES; EVAPORATED CANE JUICE SUGAR

Wholesome Sweeteners:
   www.wholesomesweeteners.com

BROWN RICE SYRUP

Lundberg Family Farms:
www.lundberg.com

VEGAN CHOCOLATE

Callebaut: *www.barry-callebaut.com*

FLOURS

King Arthur Flour:
www.kingarthurflour.com
Daisy Organic Flours:
www.daisyflour.com
Bob's Red Mill: *www.bobsredmill.com*

COCONUT OIL AND
COCONUT BUTTER

Nutiva: *www.nutiva.com*
Artisana: *www.artisanafoods.com*

VEGAN COOKIES

Zest Brands: *www.zestbrands.com*

DAIRY-FREE CHEESES

Follow Your Heart:
www.followyourheart.com
Sheese: *www.buteisland.com*
Teese: *www.chicagoveganfoods.com*

DAIRY-FREE CREAM CHEESE

Tofutti: *www.tofutti.com (always choose
a non-hydrogenated product)*

VEGAN SOUR CREAM

Tofutti: *www.tofutti.com*

VEGAN MAYONNAISE

Follow Your Heart:
www.followyourheart.com

EGG REPLACER

Ener-G: *www.ener-g.com*

EXTRACTS

Frontier: *www.frontiercoop.com*
Green Mountain Flavors:
www.greenmountainflavors.com

OTHER RESOURCES

Bob's Red Mill
A variety of grains and flours,
including almond flour, brown rice
flour, and flax seeds.
www.bobsredmill.com

King Arthur Flour
Full line of flours, including pastry,
bread, cake, whole wheat, and organic
varieties, as well as nut flours, spices,
extracts, chocolate, and cocoa powder.
www.kingarthurflour.com

Moneta
Complete line of safe non-stick
ceramic cookware.
www.gocookware.com

Nuts.com
Huge selection of nuts, dried fruit,
seeds, and flours.
www.nuts.com

Pangea
Ener-G egg replacer, agar agar, flax seed meal, vegan chocolate, tofu, and much more.
www.veganstore.com

Perelandra Natural Food Center
Large selection of natural and vegan foods, including spelt flour, vegan cream cheese, seeds, nuts, agar agar, Grade B maple syrup, and Asian ingredients.
www.perelandranatural.com

The Perfect Purée of Napa Valley
A large variety of frozen fruit purees, including passion fruit.
www.perfectpuree.com

Soya Too
Whipped soy cream.
www.soyatoo.com

Vegan Essentials
Raw food products, vegan whipped cream, vegan chocolate, arrowroot, egg replacer, and many more vegan products and staples.
www.veganessentials.com

Z Natural Foods
Raw food products, vegan chocolate, cacao butter, cocoa powder, coconut palm sugar, assorted nuts, and bulk food products.
www.znaturalfoods.com

Tips ♡ ♡ ♡ Tips ♡

♡

👑

BAKED GOODS & DESSERTS

Vegan Diva

— Always Delicious —

THANK You

ACKNOWLEDGMENTS

I've been so lucky to have the chance to be inspired in different ways by my great chef friends around the world since I started Vegan Divas in New York. Floyd Cardoz, Daniel Boulud, Eric Ripert, Laurent Tourondel, David Bouley, Ron Ben-Israel, Jacques Torres, and the 100 Best Pastry Chefs in the World—members of the Relais Dessert—whom I meet every year, including Franck Fresson, Sébastien Bouillet, and Pierre Hermé. Your passion for food inspires me.

Thanks also to:
Neil Alumkal, Milena Molina, Kacy Ewing, Felipe Saint-Martin, Felipe Coronado, Augusto Garcia, the Obsatz family, Helene Safdie, William Colaianni, Rocco Damato, and Joe Pontillo.

The HarperCollins Team, who were dedicated to this project, starting with Julie Will, executive editor—this book wouldn't exist without you. Thank you to Richard Ljoenes, Leah Carlson-Stanisic, Ashley Garland, and Stephanie Selah, for helping to make this book beautiful and get it into people's hands.

Rogério Voltan, who took the incredible photographs in this book, along with Maria Sacasa, food stylist, and Lauren Niles, prop stylist.

Tish Boyle, my cowriter, who put in a lot of hard work to make this book unique and refined in every way.

Kimberly Witherspoon and Allison Hunter, my agents.

To each and every person who supported me and continues to support me in the challenges of the business each day.

Ultimately, to my forever partner, François Payard, the most disciplined person I've ever met, whose world-renowned talent inspired me in my culinary career back in Brazil and still does every day.

INDEX

ABOUT THE AUTHOR

Fernanda Capobianco is the founder of Vegan Divas Bakery in New York City. Previously a manager and owner of the Payard Restaurant and Pastry shops in Rio de Janeiro, Fernanda translated her classic pastry skills into plant-based prowess, using healthy, organic, and fresh ingredients to create delectable desserts, sandwiches, and breakfast items at her café. Vegan Divas has been featured in publications such as *The New York Times*, *Vogue*, *New York Magazine*, *People*, and *Martha Stewart Weddings*, and is a favorite of many vegan (and vegan-leaning) celebrities, including Alicia Silverstone, Madonna, and Bethenny Frankel. Fernanda lives with her husband, pastry chef François Payard, in New York City.

Visit Fernanda on Facebook, or at www.vegandivasnyc.com.